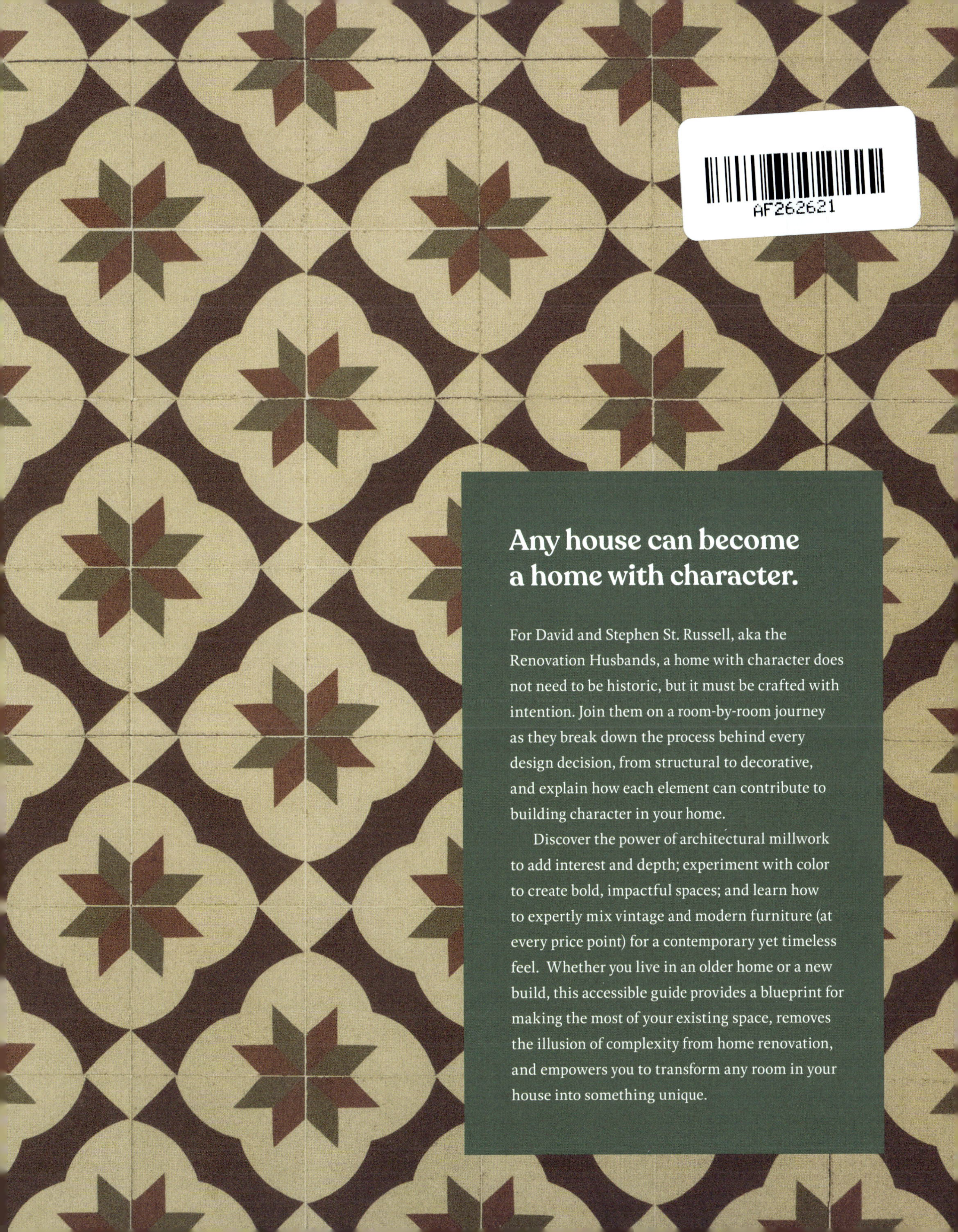

Any house can become a home with character.

For David and Stephen St. Russell, aka the Renovation Husbands, a home with character does not need to be historic, but it must be crafted with intention. Join them on a room-by-room journey as they break down the process behind every design decision, from structural to decorative, and explain how each element can contribute to building character in your home.

Discover the power of architectural millwork to add interest and depth; experiment with color to create bold, impactful spaces; and learn how to expertly mix vintage and modern furniture (at every price point) for a contemporary yet timeless feel. Whether you live in an older home or a new build, this accessible guide provides a blueprint for making the most of your existing space, removes the illusion of complexity from home renovation, and empowers you to transform any room in your house into something unique.

GOOD CHARACTER

GOOD CHARACTER

Design with Intention to Reveal Your Home's Personality

DAVID & STEPHEN ST. RUSSELL

Publisher Mike Sanders
Executive Editor Alexander Rigby
Editorial Director Ann Barton
Art & Design Director William Thomas
Designer Joanna Price
Interior Photographer Stephen St. Russell
Lifestyle Photographer Coy Sellers
Editorial Assistant Resham Anand
Developmental Editor Tiffany Taing
Copy Editor Devon Fredericksen
Proofreaders Rose Selby, Anna Wostenberg
Indexer Celia McCoy

First American Edition, 2026
Published in the United States by DK Publishing
1745 Broadway, 20th Floor, New York, NY 10019

The authorized representative in the EEA is Dorling Kindersley
Verlag GmbH. Arnulfstr. 124, 80636 Munich, Germany

Library of Congress Number: 2025950797
ISBN 978-0-5939-6872-7

DK books are available at special discounts when purchased
in bulk for sales promotions, premiums, fund-raising, or
educational use. For details, contact SpecialSales@dk.com

Printed and bound in the UK

www.dk.com

RIGHT: Our home from across the intersection
in 1929, courtesy of Historic New England.

*To our family and friends for making
us believe we could do anything,
and to the teenage versions of ourselves
for having the gumption to do it.*

Contents

FOR SALE
www.trulia.com

How It All Started

It was May 12, 2017, when we closed on our Boston Victorian and the question *What gives a home character?* began to bounce around in our heads. We left the closing, keys in hand, and headed directly to the hardware store for everything we needed to get started with cleanup. Our new home (if you could call it that) sat tall on a prominent corner and had endured years of neglect. Young and ambitious, we wanted to get started immediately and, of course, make a positive impression on our new neighbors.

Just a few months prior, we'd seen the striking, albeit run-down, 1893 Queen Anne Victorian for the first time through our car window. The home's curved bays, unique dormers, and wrap-around porch hinted at its former charm. And despite the plywood-covered windows, sagging porch, and piles of building materials scattered across the yard like a warning, we were enamored. "That would be such a cool project," we said aloud as the light turned green.

We were driving through Dorchester, Boston's largest residential neighborhood, on our way to lunch with a couple of friends who lived nearby. Up to that point, we had only visited Dorchester a handful of times, but we always found ourselves intrigued by the beautiful homes scattered throughout. It wasn't until we placed our lunch order that our friend Jesse pulled up the listing on his phone.

"Guys, you *need* to see this house."

We found ourselves poring over that vague listing, extracting any detail that would help us paint a story. We began to experience the thrill of discovering something special while simultaneously tempering the excitement in our voices. As if emoting over lunch would risk the entire dream—like declaring we'd won twenty dollars on a scratch ticket before triple checking that we hadn't made a simple mistake. After all, the road between reading a real-estate listing and homeownership is a long one.

The first photo we took as official homeowners, May 12, 2017.

We soon learned that the home had been in possession of the current owner for a short but dramatic two-year period, during which the entire interior had been stripped back to the studs. The home, now completely gutted, abandoned, and back on the market, had sat empty for months. Because of its derelict state, the home was being sold "as is," listed well below market value—and just possibly within our reach. We contacted a realtor, hoping for the chance to see inside.

It was a cold and gray winter day when we toured the home just a few days later. The interior was the kind of raw that makes your bones cold and the skin feel tight on your face. Our brains worked overtime to absorb every detail. The lathe and plaster had been removed, the plumbing and electrical stripped, and almost every original detail was missing. This place was bare, and if we were to take on this project, we would be starting from scratch.

One of the redeeming features was the original entryway and staircase, which had been spared from demolition. Victorian entries from the late 19th century were created to impress, and even in this state—dark, damp, and covered in grime—we fell in love. In the entry, a wood mantel framed the incredibly detailed teal-tile surround, an English-inspired built-in bench curved from the fireplace to the staircase, and the twisted spindles guided our eyes up to the landing, where we found the most beautiful arched original stained-glass window we had ever seen.

We submitted an offer, putting our $1,000 deposit on the line as if we were playing a game of high-stakes poker.

We were in our late twenties after all, and our threshold for risk was just as high as our grit. This home represented an opportunity to not only become homeowners in Boston but also to build something amazing together. We turned off the voices that listed all the things that could go wrong and focused on the next immediate step: Get the keys. We could work out the details later.

With the help of a government-insured mortgage, we were able to finance both the purchase of the home and the essential work needed to obtain an occupancy permit (provided by an inspector who deems a building safe to live in). Over a three-month period from June to August, we worked with a general contractor to oversee the plumbers, electricians, insulation team, floor refinishers, and plasterers. We had completed the absolute bare minimum required to obtain our occupancy permit, and we moved into our new home with the primer still drying, just happy to have walls. We spent the following months showering at the gym because we didn't have a completed bathroom and cooking on the grill because we didn't have a kitchen. None of that mattered, though, because in our minds, we had already made it.

This was one of those times in life when we were blissfully unaware of the work that lay ahead but willing to throw our entire hearts into finding out. We didn't have any idea what we were getting ourselves into and how this project—or all those to come—would help us discover what it means for a home to have *good character*.

LEFT: Sketches from our first walk-through. You can see some of our early ideas, including a half bath where the pantry currently stands.

RIGHT: Closing day—slightly overwhelmed but excited to start the exterior cleanup.

About Us

When we met, we never quite imagined we would end up *here*.

We were only teenagers, after all, when we went on our first date and fell for each other in a way only teenagers can—dreaming of being together forever but with little concept of what forever actually means. We had no idea we would watch each other graduate from college, navigate our first "real" jobs, buy our first home, get married, and abandon our corporate careers to build a business. Most of all, we never imagined we would one day be coauthoring this book.

We're from the same town in western Massachusetts, where our parents—only a couple of miles from each other—still live. We went to the same high school, and while David claims not to remember, he gave Stephen his freshman tour. David was a senior, and the difference in grade meant that we would spend the next year only vaguely familiar with each other. Casually passing in the halls, we were clueless to the fact that we would indeed spend the rest of our lives together.

David graduated in 2006 and enrolled in a nearby physician's assistant program. It wasn't until two years later that he would catch Stephen's attention again, the summer before his senior year. We went on our first date in the fall of 2008, attended Stephen's prom together the following spring, and spent that summer figuring out what would come next. Stephen had been accepted to Massachusetts College of Art and Design for architecture, and enrollment meant an inevitable move to Boston—only one year into our relationship. We pushed forward, spending Stephen's freshman and sophomore years of college crisscrossing the state, spending as much time together as possible. Somewhere along the way, we adopted our first dog, a questionable decision in retrospect, as Dexter would spend the first year of his life in split custody, handed back and forth every few weeks.

In 2011, David graduated from his master's program and made the move to Boston to start a career in medicine. We signed our first lease for a 650-square-foot dog-friendly apartment facing the Back Bay Fens, just a stone's throw from Fenway Park. A short walk through the Fens brought you to Stephen's studio, where he spent most of his time in his final years of architecture school. We only lived in that apartment for a year, but one could argue this is where this story really begins.

To the outside observer, nothing particularly eventful happened during our time in Fenway. With long days spent in the office and late nights in the studio, we began to cut grooves into our new adult lives. Stephen kept his weekly serving shift, so rent was always paid, and we spent the rest of our time enjoying the mundane. David purchased an inexpensive record player as a reward for his new job, and we spent our weekends with the windows open, allowing the sound from a record to mix with the sounds of the city just outside. There, on the deep windowsill, Dexter would doze while watching a pickup basketball game across the street.

Somewhere within the mundane, however, something

new and spectacular began to happen. We started to solve problems (of which there were many) around that small apartment. A new shelf in the postage-stamp-size kitchen, for example, or the conversion of an old coffee table into an upholstered ottoman. We painted an entire room in a single evening, and the following day, we hunted for discount curtain panels to finish the look. After completing each task, our pride of place grew, and we learned that creating a home together was something we loved.

The following summer, we received a rent-increase notice of four hundred dollars per month, forcing us to consider what was next. By then, Stephen had a year of college remaining, but we both agreed: $2,000 in rent could put a large dent in a mortgage payment for a modest home—something we could truly call our own. Armed with optimism, the energy of two young twentysomethings, and a somewhat lenient first-time home-buyers' program, we found ourselves in the (distant) Boston suburb of Walpole. There, we purchased our first home, a dated but perfectly functional 1910 property that sat stylistically somewhere between a simplified Victorian and an American Foursquare. The home had not seen an update in decades, and we moved in with a fiery enthusiasm.

By that time, our yellow lab mix, Gemma, had joined the pack, and we spent our first weekend installing a fence in the backyard. We could only afford the Gothic panels we found stacked in the parking lot of the hardware store, so we modified them by cutting off the pointed part of the picket for a more modern look. We woke up the next morning and ran to the window to make sure the fence was still standing, and that our new life wasn't just a dream.

Over the next two years, we learned the magic of doing things ourselves. We approached each task as an opportunity to add a new skill to our player card. We learned how to repair horsehair plaster, how miserable the job of stripping old woodwork is, and how to paint properly. We gutted a small bathroom and removed a wall to make it bigger. We tiled a shower for the first time and, admittedly, did a horrible job. We learned the importance of buying the right tool, but only after cheap ones gave us blisters. We built a deck, renovated a kitchen, and tiled a backsplash (doing a much better job tiling the second time around). We replaced almost thirty windows by ourselves, managing to get each install down to just three hours. We worked on that house day-in and day-out for two full years.

By 2015, now in our mid-twenties, we began to feel disconnected from our friends in the city. The market happened to be on the rise, so we took the opportunity to sell our new and improved suburban home—and in true David and Stephen fashion, we sold the house ourselves. The profit from that home changed our path—we paid off some student debt, paid for a wedding, and put some aside for our next big project.

We then signed a lease with two friends for an apartment in Boston's South End. There, seven mammals (four guys, two dogs, and one cat) shared a two-bedroom loft in a converted piano factory. During that project-free year, we planned our

*An **American Foursquare** is a two-story, box-shaped house with a square floor plan that was popular from the 1890s to the 1930s, featuring four main rooms on each floor.*

We are often asked where we learned our skill for renovation and the answer we give is the generic one: slowly, over time, and with practice. But internally we recall Walpole. The bathroom renovation, specifically, was as challenging as it was informative. Looking back on these photos, we wish for the opportunity to jump in and help, but we know that they will work it out themselves.

wedding and got married, David transitioned from practicing medicine to working in tech, and Stephen continued to navigate the corporate world of architecture and construction. Moreover, we spent the year *living*.

Everything changed in early 2017 when our roommates announced their move to the West Coast. Without them, there was no reason for us to stay in the apartment, and we suddenly faced once again the decision of what we wanted to do next: find a new, more affordable apartment, or look for a new project? That same month, on our way to lunch with two friends, we saw that striking, run-down 1893 Queen Anne Victorian through our car window . . .

Knowing this project was bigger than any of our previous undertakings, we were eager to share our process with family and friends. We created an Instagram account to document our progress, and in doing so, we discovered something far greater: an incredible community of old-house lovers. Suddenly, we had a new network of friends who offered advice, encouragement, and the motivation to persist through the harder moments. As our online community grew, so too did our sense of purpose and opportunity. Five years into our renovation, we took a leap of faith and left our corporate jobs to pursue "Renovation Husbands" full-time.

We never could have predicted where that leap would lead: from decorating the White House for Christmas, to earning the Boston Preservation Achievement Award for our Victorian, to winning an HGTV renovation competition show, to collaborating with some of the biggest and most inspiring brands along the way. We even shared a surreal afternoon with the iconic Drew Barrymore. In all, it's been an extraordinary ride and with every milestone, big or small, we remain deeply grateful.

We are writing this book in the midst of another major project: the renovation of a 1975 cabin on Maine's mid-coast. We closed on the cabin in August of 2023 while filming *Battle on the Mountain* in Colorado and split our time between that home and our Boston Victorian over the next year. These days, we spend most of our time in Maine, and with each project, we learn something new about design, perseverance, and partnership.

Reflecting on our experience, our hope is that this book offers you both practical guidance and a spark of inspiration, while helping you to uncover character in your own space. But please remember: No book or video can replace the incomparable joy that comes from shaping the place where you live with your own hands.

While there is a difference of only eight years between these photos, 2017 could not feel further away. Virtually everything about this home has changed, and in many ways, so have we.

Defining Character

"All things old were once new."

This is a phrase we picked up somewhere along the way and have never been able to shake. Over time, it began to define our core philosophy on what character is, or what it means for something to *have* character.

It's fair to say that when most people describe a home as having character, they are likely commenting on the home's age. We've all walked into an old home and said, "Oh my, this place is just bursting with character." But what does that even mean? Did the home have character when it was first built, all those years ago? Or perhaps character works like wisdom, something that's earned over time.

That leaves us with the question: *Can something new have character?*

For us, the perception of character is derived not from age but from *intentionality*—the thought, care, and craftsmanship behind every decision. That old home you walked through wasn't bursting with character simply because it was old but because it was built by craftspeople who took pride in the details. We don't always find this to be true in the modern era, leaving many of us wanting more from the homes in which we live.

So yes, we believe even something new, when shaped with intention, can be full of character.

In this book, we will start by inviting you to look more closely at your own space—its architecture, its style, and how it makes you feel—taking a moment to pause, listen to what your home has to say, and consider how its story might guide your next steps. From there, we will explore how design decisions, both big and small, can instill a sense of character into your own home.

We'll cover millwork, and how architectural details define spaces and set the scene. Then we'll explore color— how to use it with intention to elevate a mood and elicit emotion. We'll dive into the art of salvaging and thrifting, and how mixing old and new adds depth. Finally, we'll talk about furnishing and décor, and how the items you choose tell a story.

Of course, age and patina go a long way, but here we hope to take a more holistic look at the elements and principles that make you think: *this space has good character.*

The mantelpiece pulled from the basement isn't perfect. There are missing details and a cracked board, but that's okay. The imperfections are a reminder of the life it has lived and what makes it beautiful.

PART ONE
Designing
Character

KNOWING YOUR SPACE

Every home has its own starting point. You may not be starting with a gutted Victorian or a dated 1970s cabin, but each space, no matter its age or style, has something to teach you. This chapter is about learning to listen to your home, understanding its quirks and its history, and discovering the kind of character that feels most authentic to you. Through our own missteps and discoveries, we'll explore how slowing down and listening to your space can reveal exactly what it wants to become.

Our Boston Kitchen Mistake

Over the years, we've made plenty of design mistakes, but one of our earliest taught us the most. When we closed on our Boston Victorian in 2017, we only had three months remaining in our South End apartment. Those months quickly became some of the most hectic of our lives—working full-time jobs, we would sneak away to call or email various tradespeople or contractors. After work we would head to the house to do hours of labor, completing all of the prerequisites for the day to come. And finally, we would return to our apartment late in the evening, where any remaining energy would be spent dreaming of what the Victorian could one day become.

Sitting in our industrial South End loft, surrounded by exposed brick and polished concrete floors, we brainstormed ways to make our new home, dare we say, *cool*. And a Victorian shell with a sleek, contemporary interior sounded pretty cool to us. Knowing that we wouldn't have a kitchen when we moved in, we would start there, and a kitchen design was born.

When we finally moved in, our design plan and good intentions in hand, we got to work. The resulting kitchen featured a large bank of dark-gray flat-panel cabinet doors with a continuous-grain walnut feature in the center. The gray didn't end there, but continued to the island where it was capped in a large quartz waterfall counter. The fixtures were contemporary and square-cut, exactly what we were hoping for in our new space.

With the kitchen finally complete, we were thrilled with the results and incredibly proud of our work. It wasn't until we began renovating the adjacent rooms that our sensibilities shifted, and our pride gave way to unease. The kitchen we'd created felt increasingly like it didn't belong, and as we made more progress elsewhere in the house, the more it seemed to shout, "I don't fit here." What once felt exciting and new quickly became an eyesore. The kitchen was trendy in all the ways our 1893 home was timeless, and we found ourselves hating it.

We tried at length to talk ourselves down. Maybe simply swapping the cabinet doors would be enough to restore some of the missing details and charm. Maybe replacing the engineered quartz counters with a natural stone could warm and soften the setting. But the more fixes we imagined, the clearer it became: These were merely Band-Aids on a bigger problem. We decided the only way forward was to go back to the beginning.

And yes—we were frustrated with ourselves. "How could we have been so shortsighted?" we asked each other. "How did we end up in such an expensive predicament?"

LEFT: The kitchen before, during, and after our first renovation. We were so proud of what we had created, but something wasn't quite right. That may be why we lived with this almost-complete kitchen (bottom) for nearly three years.

RIGHT: A simple flat lay we created of the materials used while planning the kitchen renovation.

Boston Kitchen 2.0

We went back to the drawing board for the kitchen design in the spring of 2021, almost three years after completing it the first time. We knew that if we were going to do this project over, we couldn't afford to mess it up again. We needed to slow down and take our time.

We started by researching Victorian kitchens, not because we wanted to replicate the past, but because the past could offer clues as to what we could do better. The home's original kitchen would have been modest compared to the grander, public-facing rooms of the house. A swinging door likely would have sealed it off from guests entirely, but inside you'd find a true working kitchen.

Unlike today's built-in kitchens, Victorian kitchens were largely unfitted, meaning they were furnished with freestanding pieces, like a utilitarian sink, large oven, and sturdy worktables. The kitchen would've connected to the dining room via a "butler's pantry," which is often a small-to-medium passageway. Unlike the freestanding kitchen, the butler's pantry was *fancy* and featured floor-to-ceiling built-in cabinetry made from wood and glass. We drew a lot of inspiration from butler's pantries of the era and incorporated similar elements into our overall kitchen design.

From there, we blended what we'd learned from our research with what we knew and loved about the modern kitchen. We chose inset cabinetry to reflect the craftsmanship of the era and sourced natural materials that were available when the home was built: marble and soapstone instead of quartz, and simple brass hardware in place of more modern finishes. We opted for appliances that would be hidden behind cabinet doors so they wouldn't draw attention from the overall design. For the island, we went with cherry to contrast with the painted cabinetry, creating a more furniture-like feel—a nod to the worktables of long ago.

After months of planning, we deconstructed the former kitchen with care. We found a new home for every cabinet, counter, and appliance and started the process of implementing our new design. When we completed the project in the fall of 2022, the new kitchen became one of our proudest achievements. Now, it nestles beautifully into the aesthetic and character of our home, and we're still in love with it to this day.

LEFT: Somewhere in the learning process, you develop a better understanding of your own limitations. We knew that in order to get the kitchen of our dreams, we would need the help of a professional installer. We were saved by Ian Gardner, a master at his trade and a person we have grown to love.

Taking the Time to Listen

This process, from growing discontent with our first kitchen design to completing our second kitchen renovation, did not happen overnight. We lived with that kitchen for three years before we decided to design something new. During that period, we learned that taking the time to listen and consider the whole picture is key.

Our approach the second time around can be distilled into a simple question: *What does the house want?* No, really, we actually asked this out loud to each other. "What does the house want?"

This question became a mantra, a metaphorical guardrail to keep us in line when making design decisions. *Does this house really want a manufactured waterfall countertop?* Well, we didn't find anything like that in our research, and it doesn't *feel* quite right, so maybe not. *Does this house want a solid marble backsplash?* We didn't find examples of that specifically, but it *is* a new take on a traditional material—maybe there's something to explore there. Question after question, we challenged ideas through this new lens. After all, we did *not* want to make the same mistakes again.

Our Maine Cabin

By the time we found our Maine cabin in the fall of 2023, we'd finally learned to listen to both the house and our gut instincts. After a seven-year Victorian restoration, we were exhausted from the high-finish, built-in glossiness of it all. We were craving something looser in style, quieter, and more connected to nature. When we closed on our 1975 chalet-style cabin in Maine's midcoast, it felt like a dream come true—and an opportunity to try something new.

This project introduced a new design challenge. We weren't starting from scratch but instead with an era home that hadn't been updated in years. This house wasn't a grand historic structure asking for reverence—it was a family home with fifty years of its own nostalgia embedded in its bones. Armed with the lessons we learned in Boston, we entered this renovation with a new set of priorities. We wanted the space to feel elevated but not precious, curated but lived in, and new but as if it had always been that way.

We wanted the home to be bursting with a sense of lived-in character. *But what does character look like in a fifty-year-old cabin versus a hundred-thirty-year-old Victorian?*

For the first time, we approached the house holistically rather than one room at a time. We asked new questions, with less emphasis on style and more on the overall experience: *How does this house feel when the tide is high on a warm summer day? How does it feel when the sun sets at 4 p.m. in December? What do we want to change?* And most importantly: *What do we love exactly the way it is?*

Knowing it would take some time to become more intimate with cabin life, we put off major renovations for the first year. Instead, we focused on essentials: upgrading home systems, removing old carpets, and adding just enough paint and furniture to make the cabin comfortable. We didn't rush to decorate; we simply settled in. We spent our evenings sitting by the fire or by candlelight, experiencing the house as it moved through the seasons.

Slowing the process and taking our time to get to know the space changed everything. In that first year, the rough-sawn paneling we thought we'd paint or replace became one of our favorite features. We learned to appreciate natural woodland borders over manicured gardens. Even the 1980s-style ceiling fans, with their faux-wood blades and rattan accents, earned their keep.

Piece by piece, we began to see that character isn't defined by age or craftsmanship alone—it's found in the quirks that make a home unique. For the Maine cabin, that meant leaning into imperfection, embracing texture and warmth, and letting the house teach us what mattered most.

RIGHT: We closed on our new project while in Colorado filming HGTV's *Battle on the Mountain.* This photo was taken August 26, 2023, and to this day we have this kind of enthusiastic disbelief— our dream really did come true.

Knowing Yourself

As you read through this book and consider what your home is telling you, it's just as important to keep the other half of the equation in mind: What do *you* want?

Throughout our renovation journey, we've learned countless lessons, discovered our own style, and explored what character means to us. Our goal in sharing our experiences is to leave space for your own interpretation— space to define your taste, instincts, and story.

UNDERSTANDING HOW YOU LIVE

Before you start designing any space, we encourage you to spend time noticing your own rhythms and how you live. Where do you start your day, and where do you end it? How do you use your living room or work in your kitchen? Do you eat in the dining room or at the counter? Do you prioritize order and organization, or do you live comfortably within chaos?

Designing with intention starts by acknowledging and responding to these characteristics. If you always drop your bag on the nearest chair when you walk through your front door, maybe you don't need more discipline but a better entry solution. If your coffee mugs live on the counter because seeing them makes you happy in the morning, then perhaps that "clutter" is actually character. You don't need to change your habits to fit a design ideal. Instead, you can design around your habits.

When we moved into our Maine cabin and decided not to rush the renovation, we learned quite a few things about our routines. We observed how daylight moves through the space from the various windows, and we noticed how the living room is where we typically relaxed at the end of the day. We didn't want screens in that space, so we opted instead for a record player. The loft, in contrast, became the perfect place to watch TV before bed. Taking the time to simply live in the house gave us the chance to understand how we wanted it to feel, not just how we wanted it to look.

Drawing on lessons from our Boston kitchen, we intentionally made our Maine kitchen the last phase of our renovation. We spent two years cooking meals and spending time in the space, and our initial ideas evolved tremendously during that time. We shifted from a midcentury walnut slab to a warm oak shaker cabinet— much more in line with the cabin's feel and its existing materials. We discovered how much we loved the warm winter sunlight that poured in through the southwest-facing window. Initially, we thought we would raise the window to allow for more cabinet space, but instead we designed a cozy window seat beneath it. Finally, after hosting a holiday party, we abandoned our plan to open the kitchen to the dining room. The original division of space allowed for an intimacy we didn't want to lose—and the added benefit was that guests couldn't see the messy kitchen.

These observations resulted in a kitchen design that feels both fitted to the house and tailored to how we live within it. It's a space born not just from accumulated inspiration, but from lived experience.

The original Maine cabin kitchen and this opening were certainly charming. As we planned for the kitchen renovation, we had many, many conversations about how big would be too big for this opening in our new design.

YOU LIKE WHAT YOU LIKE

Your personal aesthetic often hides in plain sight. You already know what you're drawn to; you just might not have found the right words to describe it yet.

Do you find yourself saving images of rooms that are sparse and sculptural, or ones that feel layered and eclectic? Do you gravitate toward warm colors and cozy textures, or cool tones and clean lines? Are you energized by spaces filled with patterns, or soothed by those that are pared down and serene?

For us, that balance shifts depending on where we are. In Boston, surrounded by heavy trim and grand proportions, we leaned into refinement—structured millwork, moody paint colors, and a sense of quiet formality. In Maine, we craved something looser and more tactile: nubby fabrics, rough-sawn paneling, and the kind of imperfection that makes a room feel soft. Both approaches reflect different sides of who we are.

Your home can (and should) evolve with you. It's not about locking yourself into one aesthetic or era. It's about understanding what kinds of environments help you feel most at ease and modifying your surroundings to best fit you.

TIME WELL SPENT

What does the house want? We know it sounds intangible, even silly, but the simple question has become our most valuable design tool. The mantra turned our Victorian kitchen from a misstep into one of our proudest spaces, and it guided us in approaching the Maine cabin with patience and curiosity.

But as much as a home can guide you, the process works both ways. The other half of the equation is: *What do* you *want?* Understanding yourself—how you live and what you love—is just as vital as understanding your house. When those two perspectives align, the home begins to feel like it has real personality.

It's easy to get swept up in trends or to chase the feeling of "new." We've done it ourselves (see: Boston kitchen 1.0). But trends, by nature, move on, and what once feels fresh can quickly feel forced. The alternative isn't to reject all change—it's to shift the focus. Instead of working against your home, learn to collaborate with it. Notice what qualities feel timeless and what quirks give it charm. By tuning in to what you want *and* what the house wants, you can create spaces that feel both true to the home's bones and deeply personal to you.

LEFT: We may be in the minority, but we love heat from an old-fashioned cast-iron radiator—we just don't always love how they look. This built-in helped with the awkward curve of the bay window while hiding the radiator, providing additional storage and, of course, a warm place to sit.

QUESTIONS TO CONSIDER

If what the house wants isn't clear right away, here are
some questions that can help you get to the core of the idea:

What is the architectural style of your home?

There are several home styles (Craftsman, Greek Revival, and
Tudor, for example), and each one comes with a set of "rules"
or guidelines that define it. This includes elements such as
proportions, molding profiles, decorative motifs, and more. If you
live in a specific style of home as we do, then it's really helpful to
familiarize yourself with those basic characteristics. It's your choice
to either embrace the style or select elements that contrast with it,
but it's always helpful to understand the context.

Where do you live?

The location of your house can tell you a lot more about your home
than you may think! Traditionally, homes from specific regions
have their own vernacular, or a common language of form and
design. A small home on Cape Cod is going to look quite different
from the same small home in the Midwest, for example. Homes are
often built to reflect their use, the population they serve, and the
materials available. Take a drive around your area to find houses
with similar architectural styles, and you'll start picking up on the
patterns, ensuring your home nestles well into your neighborhood.

What do you want the house to feel like?

Not what style, but how do you want it to feel? Or better yet, how
does it feel? If you already love your home for a specific feeling or
vibe it gives you, use that as a guide for your future interventions.
Similarly, if your goal is to try to make your home feel a certain
way, run your design decisions through that lens. In the Maine
cabin, one of our goals is to maintain and elevate the cabin-like
aesthetic we love so much. Pair that with our interest in capturing
a 1970s retro vibe, and it starts to paint a picture of how we want
the house to feel.

MILLWORK

Architectural details set the tone for how a space is experienced, and millwork can bring warmth and craftsmanship into otherwise unfinished spaces. From the very first room we ever designed, we always consider the architecture first. In this chapter, we will explore how proportion, style, and scale create visual harmony—and how trim, whether ornate or simple, can add character to every room.

Filling in the Gaps

When we moved into our Boston Victorian, the walls were new, skimmed with a thin layer of plaster, and sealed with a fresh coat of primer. In anticipation of adding trim, the walls were intentionally left rough-cut at the bottom. The resulting irregular gap ran just a couple of inches above the floor, allowing light to sneak in from the basement below. Trim is not a prerequisite for obtaining an occupancy permit, so it wasn't a priority for us before moving in, and the task of installing it was left to us.

Which begged the question: *How exactly were we going to restore the craftsmanship that was missing in this house?*

We were overwhelmed by the possibilities—and by just how much trim our home would need. Without the budget to replicate historic profiles or to hire a professional, we knew we'd be tackling the work ourselves. For clues on how to move forward, we turned to our partially intact entryway. Reaching into our bag of samples, we discovered that many modern profiles are rooted in designs over a century old. Piece by piece, we studied what remained: the height of the baseboards and the panels above them, the curve of the base cap, the shape of the apron beneath the window stool, and the characteristics of the door and window casings. One by one, we matched each detail with a contemporary counterpart, gradually sketching out a blueprint for the entire house. Suddenly, the task felt possible—we could make this work.

For our new walls, instead of taping and mudding each seam, we opted for plaster. While technically part of a higher (and more expensive) skill set, plastering takes a fraction of the time. The entire home was drywalled and plastered within a couple of days. Here you can see the unique sheen of a plaster finish and the start of floor repairs.

We understand that most people are not starting from scratch. If you look around your home, there's likely plenty of trim already installed, and plenty of room for improvement, too. Whether you live with "builder-grade" finishes, the aftermath of a bad renovation, or simply a space that feels flat and unfinished, this chapter is for you. Improving the architectural details of your home can profoundly shape how your space is experienced. It is also one of the best ways to add architectural character to your home.

TIP: We had a breakthrough moment in our planning when we decided to build a miniature trim mockup using samples (above, right). This helped us to see how all the pieces would fit together, allowing us to tinker with trim size or spacing until we liked the feel. Before we knew it, we were ready to start installing millwork, one room at a time.

The curved bays of an old Victorian can be quite tricky. Traditionally, crown molding and window trim were made with a plaster mold. However, we found that our lumberyard could produce a rubber-like version of any profile. In the dining room, we used these flexible pieces instead for the top of the window casings and the curves of the bay, which somehow blended perfectly with the wood profiles.

What Is Millwork?

"Millwork" refers to any wood products that are traditionally manufactured in a mill and used in building construction or interior design. This includes moldings, doors, windows, staircases, built-ins, and decorative woodwork. Casually, we sometimes refer to millwork as "trim."

WE BLAME THE QUEEN

Was it Queen Victoria (1837–1901) who was responsible for all the fuss over trim? Well, Queen Victoria didn't personally design ornate buildings, but her reign popularized over-the-top architectural styles we now refer to as "Victorian." During a time of industrial innovation and nostalgia for the romantic, she embraced revivalist design (think Gothic castles) and effectively rebranded ornamentation as a symbol of progress, prosperity, and pride.

Our 1893 Boston Victorian is more specifically considered a Queen Anne Victorian, a style that became common at the tail end of the Victorian era, around the 1880s in the United States. This style of home, considered the pinnacle of opulence during its peak, is asymmetrical and features steep roofs with gables and turrets, wrap-around porches, and ornate details. It was eclectic at the time, and very popular, so much so that our Boston neighborhood has hundreds of them. Throw a rock in any direction, and you will hit a Queen Anne Victorian, and maybe even shatter a stained-glass window in the process. The irony is that our entire neighborhood was built over a single decade by just a handful of builders. We sometimes joke that we live in one of the earliest American subdivisions.

THEY DON'T MAKE THEM LIKE THEY USED TO

It wasn't until the early 20th century that American homes began their shift away from the ornate Victorian interiors of the late 1800s to something simpler. The vibe was new, and Victorian interiors suddenly started to feel, well, excessive. The cost of labor was on the rise, as was the ease of large-scale manufacturing. As a result, American architecture saw the introduction of new styles like Colonial Revival and Arts & Crafts, among others, that were a direct result of the subsequent machine-led manufacturing era. Cost-cutting during the Great Depression simplified homes even further, and this trend of simplification continued. By the postwar housing boom of the 1940s and the growing influence of midcentury-modern design, homes began to feature the simplest trim possible—and sometimes none at all.

Fast forward to the early 2000s, when we were coming of age during the McMansion era. We still remember visiting friends who lived in these new, large suburban homes and being in awe of their sheer size and open floor plans. Unfortunately, we later recognized that many of these homes were built to prioritize speed and profit over detail. This resulted in subdivisions that looked copied and pasted, generally lacking uniqueness and detail. The trim was undersized and had that ordinary off-the-shelf feeling, leaving much to be desired.

If you live in one of these "contractor grade" homes, hope is not lost. Millwork and architectural details profoundly shape how a space is experienced and can be added to any home!

Stephen took these photographs while on a winter walk. The homes are all unique and stand like beautiful giants. Fun fact: the top left photo shows the previous home of the Knight brothers of New Kids On The Block. We literally live on *the* block.

Getting Started with Millwork

We both remember the first time we entered our local lumberyard. Because it was only open during the most inconvenient times, we waited for a workday where we could both play hooky. We made the journey from Dorchester to Cambridge, which, if you are unfamiliar, is no small feat. As we approached the industrial park, we scanned the poorly marked buildings for any sign of direction, eventually finding ourselves parked and working up the courage to go inside. "Um, hello, do you sell to homeowners?"

That visit turned out to be the first of many. We quickly got to know the staff and familiarized ourselves with the process. We learned how to navigate the profile catalog, locate our selections within the racks, request pieces to be cut to size, and made full use of the generous sample wall. Compared to the big-box stores, the quality of the trim was higher, the options broader, and the prices lower. Discovering the magic of a lumberyard completely shifted our perspective on what was possible.

Even if you're not ready to start a project, a quick visit to the lumberyard can offer much inspiration, almost like a mood board of millwork options. Pick up a catalog, grab some samples, and get a feel for the selection. Sometimes, just holding those pieces in your hands is enough to get the wheels turning.

TIP: Whenever someone asks us where to source wood or milled products, we always recommend starting at the lumberyard or, if there isn't a local option, exploring the many online suppliers that ship nationwide.

BULFINCHES

Before you begin adding millwork to your space, it helps to understand your home's intended style. Maybe you live in a Craftsman, a Colonial, or a condo with no clear identity. Most architectural styles are naturally complemented by a specific set of trim profiles, and catalogs are often organized by collections with these styles in mind. With a little research, you can uncover which profiles were historically designed for your type of home. (See "Questions to Consider" at the end of the chapter for a deeper dive.)

Once you've done this, take a moment to create an inventory of the trim already found throughout your home. Does it align with your home's original style? Is it consistent throughout? In many homes, older areas may still carry that historic detail, while updated or renovated areas may introduce something new. Every home has its own story, and inconsistencies are common.

From this point, you have the opportunity to form your own vision. Does your home feel cohesive and intentional? Are there some areas that really need help? Ultimately the choice to add or replace trim is up to you. You can follow tradition, mix styles, or create a trim language that is completely your own. The key is to be intentional about your decisions and apply those decisions or rules consistently throughout your home moving forward.

OPPOSITE, TOP: The renovation of the third floor changed everything. Not only were we able to deviate from the strict Victorian style of the floors below, but we created functional spaces that changed the way we use our home. The third floor feels like a portal into a lighter, brighter, and more relaxed world.

OPPOSITE, BOTTOM: Nothing has been more fun than exploring brand-new styles like this 1970s-inspired dining room in our Maine cabin. While it has continued to evolve, it will always have that retro flair.

ABOVE: In the Boston Victorian primary suite, we explored ways to elevate the trim and differentiate it from the guest bedrooms. We were inspired to create this window detail by Daniel Kanter—who wrote a blog post on the topic years prior—and it never left us.

A NOTE ON SCALE

While you begin to develop your own trim language, it's important to consider scale. Trim collections often offer multiple size options for each trim profile. For example, the door casing we selected for our Boston Victorian comes in small, medium, and large variations. For homes with ten-plus-foot ceilings, the scale is much different from one with eight-foot ceilings, and we took this detail into consideration when making our selection. Oversized trim in a small space can make that space feel smaller, whereas dinky trim (as we like to call it) in a large space can make the millwork feel like an afterthought. The key is to play with the proportions of your space to make it feel right-size.

You can also adjust the scale from room to room based on that room's function. It's very common in historic homes to put the largest and most expensive trim on the first floor, as the "hosting rooms," like the parlor, living room, and dining room, are typically located there. As you head upstairs to the bedrooms and bathrooms, the trim likely scales back to a more modest profile. If you have a third floor, you may notice a further reduction in size and quality.

We considered this cascading trim size while developing our plan and decided that both the first and second floors could support the larger door casings, baseboards, and crown molding. Beyond scale, this was a strategic decision, as the price increase for the larger selections was nominal, and now the same profiles could be used throughout the house, simplifying our renovation process.

In the Maine cabin, the existing trim shared the same scale throughout the entire home. Basic three-and-a-half-inch pine boards were routed by hand to feature a large radius. This profile appears over and over—for the baseboards, the doors, and the windows. As we renovated each room, we resisted the urge to modify the size or scale of the trim, instead leaning into what was already in place, and we love how it turned out. The scale is appropriate for the eight-foot ceilings there, and the simplified detail lends itself to a classic 1970s cabin.

REPAIRING EXISTING MILLWORK

If you own an older home, you likely have enough millwork in your space to get you started. Experience tells us that your millwork is also likely caked in decades of paint, and probably even some lead. You will have to decide if you want to start the journey of stripping the paint and restoring the natural wood (the most difficult option), stripping back the paint to repaint over it (easier), or replacing it altogether (expensive). We won't lie—all these options are miserable. Our advice: Take your time to decide which path is right for you, start with one room, and get really into audiobooks.

If you have your original trim and it's not painted, congratulations! You have won the trim lottery. While we can't technically tell you what to do, please don't paint it. Lean into the natural wood.

It's hard to describe the level of joy you experience at this point in the project. All of the dirty work is over: the woodwork is done, the nail holes are filled, and the gaps are caulked. A fresh coat of paint makes the patched-up woodwork feel clean and cohesive, which gives you the first glimpse at how the finished space will really look. And if we're being honest, we nailed the proportions in this room.

Millwork Applications

RISE OF THE OPEN FLOOR PLAN

Sometime in the late 1990s to early 2000s, the general population decided that bigger means better. McMansions were multiplying like rabbits, and inside them, the advent of the infamous open floor plan became the norm. Houses were designed with massive rooms that encompassed the kitchen, dining room, and living room all in one. This epidemic was so pervasive that the idea spread into home renovation, with walls demoed and rooms conjoined without much thought to how that might alter the experience of living in such spaces. Support beams have truly never worked harder than they have in the open-floor-plan era.

In truth, we don't disagree with the concept outright. Times change, and homes should change along with them. Plus, modern homes need modern solutions. People no longer value a formal sitting room to contrast their informal living rooms, and current trends no longer conceal kitchens. Our priorities have shifted to be multipurpose and informal, and we think that's great! Creating open spaces allows for cross-conversation, convenient means of entertaining, and easy circulation.

Somewhere along the way, however, form began to outweigh function, and we lost the thread. The priority became *bigger* spaces over *efficient* spaces. Practically speaking, these open and oversized rooms are really difficult to design within because they lack clear delineations. They are also really difficult to furnish because everything appears to be floating in space—and there is nothing cozy about that. More than anything, these large open rooms tend to lack character.

When we first walked into our gutted Boston Victorian, we were faced with the opportunity to reconfigure the first floor entirely. So we asked ourselves, "What will we keep open and what should we close off?"

CASED OPENINGS

As we looked to strike a happy medium between open and closed spaces, the key to our success was the cased opening. Put simply, a cased opening is a framed architectural opening between two rooms that has finished molding but no door. These openings can vary in size, from a standard thirty-inch door to upwards of eight feet. Rather than having one large, continuous space, a cased opening allows for the creation of two distinct spaces without completely closing them off from each other. This division allows for two rooms with independent identities that still remain connected.

In the Boston Victorian, we decided to take the once standard doorways between each room and make them larger. We connected the parlor to the dining room and the living room (featured on the cover of this book). With five new large openings, there was plenty of opportunity for circulation, sight lines, and dispersed sunlight, all while providing a termination point for each room's individual design.

BASEBOARDS AND CROWN MOLDING

We like to start our millwork journey with the baseboard
because it is the most common of all trim. Baseboard
is used to bridge the bottom of the wall and the floor.
Traditionally, baseboards are installed *before* the hardwood
floor is in place, but this process has long since changed to
reduce the labor required to create perfectly fitted floors. In
builder-grade homes, the baseboard is often quite small and
generally lacking in detail. This simplification was achieved
by taking more detailed profiles and shrinking them down
to fit on a single board—like those you will find at the
hardware store. If you're looking for something more than
a basic baseboard, creating a two-piece baseboard might be
the solution. This entails installing a flat board and adding a
detailed base cap on top.

Crown molding sits at the opposite end, bridging the
wall and the ceiling. It is the most complicated trim to
install but adds an often important layer of finish to the
space. Crown is available in a wide variety of sizes, from a
small and simple profile to large multipiece options. For the
Boston Victorian, we used a large crown, and in the Maine
cabin, we opted for a small, simplified crown, or at times, no
crown at all.

PICTURE-FRAME MOLDING

Picture-frame molding is an ornamental wall treatment
applied directly to the wall to create a series of rectangular
or square boxes resembling a picture frame. This practice
dates back to the Georgian period of the 1700s, when

*__Shoe molding__ is a piece of molding that is sometimes
added to the baseboard to cover up larger gaps along
the floor. Shoe molding is one of our least favorite types
of trim, as it points to the prioritization of speed over
craftsmanship. If shoe molding is required, we suggest
trying something more creative than a quarter round.*

plaster became a popular method of adding detail to homes. Sometimes also referred to as "wall framing" or "box trim" (not to be confused with wainscoting), picture-frame molding adds visual interest and a touch of grandeur to any room.

Looking through your millwork catalog, you will likely find a section on "panel molding" with profiles that are one to two inches wide and that taper down on both sides. When applying the molding, the shallower taper should be on the inside of the square. What you want to avoid when selecting picture-frame molding are profiles actually intended for panel details or base caps. This is a common mistake because such profiles are more readily available at big-box stores, but it just isn't correct.

When it comes to choosing proportions for your picture-frame molding, things become a bit trickier. Every room is unique, and there are no hard-and-fast rules, but it's important to achieve both balance and emphasis. To do this, consider the reason you're installing the molding: Do you want to break up a long hallway? (Equal-size boxes may do the trick.) Are you trying to highlight a specific piece of art or furniture? (Consider opting for a large box flanked by smaller ones.) Or are you looking for something else entirely?

In any case, we recommend planning the entire layout by applying painter's tape right to the wall in various picture-frame proportions to help visualize your design options—then spending a few days living with it, making any adjustments as needed.

Adding picture-frame molding to our Boston Victorian parlor allowed us to emphasize important items like our piano and grandmother clock.

CHAIR-RAIL MOLDING

Chair-rail molding serves as a horizontal belt around the middle of the room, cutting the walls into upper and lower sections. Traditionally, this piece of trim kept furniture from damaging the plaster wall upon contact. Nowadays, we tend to use this detail in combination with picture-frame molding to help break up the wall and to avoid picture frames from becoming too tall. Remember, there are no hard-and-fast rules—and this level of detail may not be necessary in your home, so don't forget to refer back to your plan and home style!

PICTURE-RAIL MOLDING

Picture-rail molding is a more niche piece of millwork, but it can pack a dramatic punch when implemented into your space. These moldings are shaped to allow hooks to latch onto them so you can hang pictures without disturbing the wall coverings or the delicate plaster. This profile sits closer to the top of a wall and sometimes doubles as the crown molding. The next time you're in an older home, take a moment to look at the crown molding—if there is a shadow line along the top, it may actually be picture-rail molding!

ABOVE: The picture-rail molding not only helped break up this two-tone room, but also served as a great spot to hang things from, such as this mirror, or chain of monkeys.

OPPOSITE: This Boston Victorian parlor demonstrates many trim uses. While this photo highlights the picture-frame and chair-rail molding, you can also see the baseboard and base-cap profiles, crown, window casing, and cased opening. The placement of the existing light switch was unfortunate, but we made it work.

The word "paneling" is a broad term because it refers to many applications. It ranges from traditional wainscoting found in our Boston Victorian entryway to simple pine tongue-and-grooves featured throughout the Maine cabin. Whatever the level of detail or complexity you're looking for, the goal of paneling is the same: to provide a sense of customization, texture, and detail through a decorative wall treatment.

Our first soiree into paneling was inspired by a visit with our neighbor. Their Victorian home is not dissimilar to ours, and we were both immediately taken when we entered their dining room. The original paneling is a deep-brown wood that extends to cover the bottom two-thirds of the walls. The scale and level of detail make the space feel important and intentional. It has so much character.

When approaching our own space, we pulled out our catalog of profiles and began to model each panel. We built them in the basement, one by one, and installed them in the dining room. Not yet having the skill set to create flawless panels, we opted for paint over a natural wood finish. The end result made the dining room feel timeless, weighted in space, and intentional.

TOP: In our Boston Victorian primary suite, we added paneling to one wall in order to anchor the bed. The roof-line cutting through the room made for a unique panel shape that adds interest— and took us hours to optimize.

BOTTOM: In the Maine cabin, a simpler version of paneling wraps many of our spaces. While simpler to plan and install, it still has a huge impact.

BUILT-INS

When we started on our Boston Victorian parlor, we spent months sketching designs. The room is mostly round, as it follows the shape of our wrap-around porch, making it very challenging to furnish. We thought of every possible configuration, from ordering a custom curved couch to using two sectionals and more—we really considered it all. Then it dawned on us, the problem with the room wasn't the awkward shape (entirely)—it was the scale. The scale was too large to create the intimate space we were dreaming of. The solution? Built-in bookcases.

We ditched our plan (or lack thereof) and started anew. We decided to design a large built-in that would consume an entire wall, making sure it would be deep enough for cabinets to run along the bottom. This built-in would deepen the cased opening and, in the process, create a finished portal that would serve as a buffer between two distinct spaces, inviting your eye to peer through.

When the built-in was finally installed, everything changed. The scale of the room was reduced to the appropriate size, and the coziness of the parlor we were hoping for clicked into place.

Built-ins can be used in a ton of ways, from framing a central fireplace to filling a small nook or encasing an unsightly radiator. Their bespoke nature makes for endless possibilities, allowing you to showcase your belongings and tell your story. In short, they are opportunities for character.

We worked with a local craftsman, Ken DeCost, to help with both of these built-ins. They both house radiators and contain functional storage.

QUESTIONS TO CONSIDER

The world of millwork is a big one, and offers a myriad of ways to add character to your home. Here are a few things to consider when approaching this design element:

What architectural language does your home speak?

"Architectural language" can mean a few things. As we discussed in Knowing Your Space, if your home has a defined architectural style, use that as a starting point for choosing millwork profiles that align with it. Many millwork companies offer style-specific catalogs (Craftsman, Greek Revival, Colonial Revival, etc.) that can serve as helpful guardrails to ensure what you add feels authentic to your home's original character.

More simply, architectural language can also refer to repeating elements. Is there a detail in your home that you love? Consider echoing it elsewhere to create continuity throughout the entire home. For example, the original bench seats in the living room of our Maine cabin have a chunky, rounded edge that feels perfectly cabin-like, so we decided to carry that same shape to our kitchen shelves and window bench seat. Small gestures like this can make new features feel as though they've always belonged.

What's the scale of your home— and your rooms?

Are your ceilings eight feet high or lower? Or are your rooms large and double height? Considering the scale of your spaces helps determine not only what size your trim profiles should be but also how you might use millwork (like applied moldings or built-ins) to make the proportions feel balanced and intentional.

How "finished" does your home feel right now?

Stand in each room and notice where your eyes rest. Do the walls "end" gracefully, or do they stop abruptly? Consider where added detail could bring a sense of completion: crown molding to draw the eye upward, a casing to define an opening, or a baseboard to ground the room. Remember, millwork isn't just decoration— it's punctuation. Does your space lack a focal point that could be enhanced through trim or architectural detail?

What vibe do you want your rooms to evoke?

For instance: ornate, minimalist, studious, grand, neutral? When we think about styling a room, we often start with finishes, color, and décor—but adjusting or adding millwork can be the most powerful way to influence how a space feels architecturally, not just materially.

COLOR

Few design elements offer such substantial return for relatively little effort as adding color. Color plays a defining role in how a space feels, and painting is one of those projects where a single weekend's work can completely transform a space. In this chapter, we'll explore how to use paint, finish, and texture to create harmony throughout your home. From developing a cohesive palette to understanding undertones and sheen, color is your most accessible tool for creating spaces that feel truly *you*.

Color Is Complicated

When designing a space, one of the first things you'll naturally want to consider is color: the color of the walls, the ceiling, the trim, and even the décor you'll curate. And the number of choices, especially if you don't do this type of design often, can quickly become overwhelming.

When one of our good friends bought their first house, our text messages suddenly shifted from random memes to home questions and how-tos:

> **Friend:** "Okay, I have watched enough YouTube that I think we can replace the toilet ourselves, but what color should I paint the bathroom?"
> **Us:** "You can totally replace your own toilet . . . As for the color, well, that's a bit trickier."

We were happy to offer our suggestions, but we did so with a caveat: We have picked a lot of colors in our day, but never for *their* house. And while we are happy to help on a number of topics, choosing specific colors is more challenging. There is truly no substitute for being in a space. This isn't the easiest to explain when you've become the "DIY friend" and everyone is looking for your opinion and expertise.

Instead, we like to recommend starting your color journey by looking for inspiration in spaces similar to your own, and with a healthy amount of sampling. Color is incredibly subjective—what we personally find to be the "perfect" color, you might find to be horrendous. Choosing color is about finding what is right for you, and for your home.

Over the course of our renovation journey, we've developed an understanding about how color can transform a space, how light affects color, how sheen changes perception, and how creating palettes that feel cohesive and timeless are key to building character. These are some of the things you will want to consider to feel confident when selecting a color that's right for you.

A few weeks after our color conversation, our friend sent a photo of their bathroom, toilet installed and lots of paint swatches on the wall:

> **Friend:** "Omg, there are too many different shades of white."
> **Us:** "Lol—we completely agree—way too many."

LEFT: The Boston Victorian living room was the first room completed after the kitchen. The bold color and trim profiles really set the tone for the rest of the first floor.

RIGHT: The color plan for the Boston Victorian's ground floor.

Developing a Home Color Palette

Whether you have already painted a few rooms in your house or are starting from square one, creating a whole-home color palette is a great exercise to make your spaces feel cohesive. And listen, we get it—choosing colors for individual rooms is hard enough, let alone for your entire house. But we challenge you to take on the task of thinking about your home holistically.

LOOK WITHIN YOUR HOME

What are the existing materials and fixtures in your home that your chosen colors will be paired against? This might include flooring, wall treatments, cabinetry, wood trim, furniture, and even your favorite art or textiles. These are the elements that will likely remain as constants throughout the renovation, and you'll want your new color palette to play nicely with them.

CREATE A MOOD BOARD

Our entire approach to design changed when we started creating mood boards, and they've since become an integral part of our process. It's the perfect way to collect all your ideas in one easy-to-reference place—and a method for showcasing existing finishes and furniture next to new color swatches. We tend to start this process digitally, making it easy to rapidly iterate and brainstorm. But the same process can be done with physical swatches, paper, and sketches!

For our Maine cabin, we created a mood board to help us establish a whole-home look and feel. We started by adding photos of existing elements, like the rough-sawn wood walls, with inspirational images we'd collected online. We explored textures, colors, and finishes and compiled them all in one place. From there, we created a new mood board for each room in the home. It's been a great way to explore and narrow down options before moving to physical swatches, and a great place to return to if we ever lose focus.

LEFT: A simple mood board created in Canva to help visualize a mixture of existing materials and new materials/colors that we hope to use throughout the home. We return to this visual before introducing anything new.

RIGHT: Nothing is more helpful than large physical swatches. We used foam core boards and painted them ourselves, moving them around the house to see the color in different lighting.

Referencing your mood board, begin by considering what your "anchor" color might be. This color will most likely be a light neutral or a white that you can repeat throughout your home, helping each space feel cohesive. This is especially true in homes with large open spaces. In the Maine cabin, we took the existing materials into consideration—the dark rough-sawn wood walls, the golden pine feature walls, and the light wood floors—when selecting our warm-white anchor. We have now used that color extensively—on every ceiling, and throughout the first floor.

You will quickly find, as our friend did, that choosing white paint can be a lot harder than it sounds. All white colors have an undertone—some lean blue, while others may lean more yellow or pink. They will all look "white" in the paint can, but once you start swatching (testing paint samples on your walls in small batches), their differences will become evident. One of our favorite tips is to pick up free color chips at the hardware store and bring the color chip into the room you plan to paint, taped to the center of a piece of computer paper. This will allow you to see the neutral color in contrast to pure white and help to reveal the undertone in the room!

Your ideal anchor color should complement the existing materials in your home, and pair well with your other color selections. So remember to keep your anchor color on hand (and on your mood board) as you explore more saturated colors to contrast with it.

ABOVE: When our kitchen cabinets arrived, our specified color (Accessible Beige) was slightly off from what we imagined, but we liked it even better. Our new color, which we named "Barbara," was born from a color match and became the trim color throughout the space. It pairs beautifully with Alabaster, which became our Boston Victorian anchor color.

RIGHT: We said, "1970s equals avocado," and we love it. Never judge a color by its first coat.

CHOOSING COLOR

Whether part of a whole-home palette or as a one-off, choosing a color can be daunting. Color is subjective (as it should be!), so we are not going to tell you what colors you should or should not be using. The goal here is to choose colors that make *you* happy. Here are a few places you can start:

+ Choose colors you already love or that you have saved along the way. Use a fan deck or online tools to explore similar or complementary colors. You can purchase a fan deck at your hardware store. Additionally, many paint brands will provide suggestions for natural complements on their website.

+ Reference historical color palettes. Most paint brands have curated color collections derived from historic colors or specific eras. Our go-tos are Benjamin Moore's Williamsburg collection and Sherwin-Williams's midcentury palette—both of which we referenced for our Maine cabin.

+ Follow interior-design creators and bloggers. Most are very generous in sharing their design process and have paint colors listed on their websites and social media.

+ Collect magazines and design books—a great way to find curated color inspiration in a variety of styles. Some design books (including this one!) will even include a resources appendix that shares the paints and finishes featured in the book.

+ Finally, Pinterest. There is no better online tool to find inspiration and to save references for future projects.

When you start bringing colors into the "real world" by swatching or painting a room, you may find that they look different from what you expected. This is especially true with white because of its various shades and sheens, but it occurs with all colors. Maybe you're trying out a color you found online or in your friend's house, or maybe it's one you've used before.

In our first home, we painted our entryway Revere Pewter—a light, warm gray that suited the space perfectly. The color was very popular at the time, and we loved it. Years later, when choosing a color for our guest bathroom in our Boston Victorian, we didn't even question it: "Revere Pewter would be perfect here!" we agreed. But after we painted the first wall, something felt very wrong to us. "Is this the same color? It looks like poop." We asked ourselves: *What changed?*

The difference was the lighting. In the entryway of our first home, all the windows faced southwest, flooding the space with natural light. In the guest bathroom of the Boston Victorian, there was only a small east-facing window that overlooked a large green tree. In short, the small room got very little natural light.

The cardinal direction of your windows, and the resulting quality and temperature of the light, dramatically affects how colors appear in the space. And because sunlight shifts throughout the day and the year, the same paint color you loved in one space can look entirely different in another room. It's important, then, to understand where your light is coming from:

+ **South**-facing rooms receive warm, direct light throughout the day, making colors appear brighter and more vivid.

+ **East**-facing rooms glow warmly in the morning but cool off later in the day. Colors may appear vibrant in the morning, then may look dull or drab in the evening.

+ **North**-facing rooms get indirect cooler light throughout the day that can mute lighter tones and deepen dark ones.

+ **West**-facing rooms begin cool and dim, then flood with warm light in the evening.

Considering the orientation of the windows throughout your home will help you not only in selecting color candidates but also in understanding how your chosen color will shift throughout the day and the seasons. In the summer, golden light and green foliage can make tones appear warmer, while the cool skies and bare trees of winter can mute them. Of course, we're not suggesting you need to coordinate your colors with the seasons, but it helps to explain why the deep green you loved in July might look a bit different by January.

This is the Boston Victorian second-floor guest bathroom. The room is prettiest in the morning when the sun pours in. The rest of the day, however, this room is dark—a consideration when choosing the paint color and materials.

A NOTE ON CONTRAST

We have never been fans of high-contrast color schemes. The very popular combination of Hale Navy (a dark blue) and Pure White trim immediately comes to mind—and it's not our preference. If your home palette contains a lot of deep, bold colors, there are so many other pairing options than ultra-bright white. Opting for a complementary off-white reduces the overall contrast and makes the space feel more intentional.

We learned this lesson in contrast early. When we painted the living room of our Boston Victorian a deep green-blue, we found that our eye got "stuck" on the line where the wall met the ceiling. For us, the high-contrast paint scheme was too bright and too distracting.

We took out our fan deck and found a complementary light green-gray as an alternative. The outcome was both dramatic and somewhat uneventful. The decrease in contrast elevated the overall feeling of the room and added to the warmth we were seeking in the space, but the ceiling still very much looked white. It's a subtle detail, but it makes a big difference.

All this to say, keep in mind that there are more options than just bright white when painting your ceiling or trim. Still, at the end of the day, you know what you like best in your own home—high contrast or not.

LEFT: The ceiling here may look white, but in contrast to the bright curtains, you can see how warm the color actually is.

RIGHT: These color swatches helped us compare the two room colors with true white.

COLOR DRENCHING

Sometimes referred to as "tone-on-tone," painting an entire room (walls, trim, and ceiling) in a single hue has become increasingly popular in recent times, and we love to see more people experimenting with the concept. Often, this design choice is associated with the use of more saturated (darker) colors but can also include neutrals.

When designing our Boston Victorian parlor, we researched similar historical rooms and learned that color drenching is more than just a new trend—it draws inspiration from the maximalism of historic English interiors. These grand estates often boasted saturated libraries, parlors, and drawing rooms. The pigment required to achieve these vibrant colors was expensive, and the practice was meant to show off wealth.

In the parlor, we chose a deep green for the walls, trim, built-ins, and of course, the ceiling. The new color instantly made the room feel special by distinguishing it from the adjoining spaces. The deeply saturated color changed the scale of the room, making it feel more intimate, and facilitated the cozy atmosphere we were trying to evoke.

When working with lighter colors, like in our Boston Victorian kitchen and throughout our Maine cabin, we always prefer to color drench. Color drenching allows your eyes to flow smoothly and uninterrupted throughout the space. Without a change in color where the walls meet the ceiling, the room will feel larger. Bonus: The task of painting becomes easier when there is no need to cut in or tape off!

The often-overlooked key to color drenching is using sheen (instead of color) to create visual interest and contrast. In our parlor, we applied semi-gloss paint on the built-ins, crown molding, baseboard, and chair-rail molding, helping those elements to stand out against the flat-finished walls. And after a short debate, we opted to paint the picture-frame molding with the flat finish to match the walls. This allowed the picture-frame molding to feel like a natural part of the wall's texture rather than something that was applied on top. This hierarchy of sheen gives a room painted with a single color a surprising depth and sophistication.

TIP: If you are not ready to color drench a room or you are looking for a less dramatic option, consider painting the ceiling the same color but in a lower saturation. While purchasing the paint, you can specify your percentage of pigment. For example, you can request "Colonial Verdigris at 70%," which will result in a slightly lighter color while maintaining the same hue.

Color drenching the Boston Victorian parlor lends itself to the analog space we were looking to create. This is the perfect spot to put on a record and vibe.

Choosing Paint and Sheen

Color is one thing—choosing paint is another entirely. We are often asked which brand of paint is our favorite, and we typically respond with: "It doesn't matter much." You are likely limited to the paint brands at your local hardware store, and they are all completely fine. With more experience, you may develop specific brand preferences, as we have, but that comes with time. If you're unsure, rely on your hardware store to guide you toward the correct product for your specific application.

Once you have picked the product, the next thing to consider is sheen. And please bear with us while we discuss sheen—because we have *strong* feelings on the topic. Each time you approach a paint counter, you will be asked to choose a paint sheen, or the level of shininess. The most common options, from least shiny to most shiny, are: flat, matte, eggshell, satin, semi-gloss, gloss, and high-gloss. Each option lends itself to a different application, but like color, sheen is *technically* subject to preference.

We once overheard a customer consult the paint clerk on what sheen he recommended for walls. "Eggshell," the clerk advised. "It's basically the same as matte, and it is the best." As our souls left our bodies, we looked at each other and fought the urge to jump over the counter in protest. They are *not* the same, and in this section, we intend to tell you why we feel so strongly about the topic.

TIP: If you are stuck choosing between satin, semi-gloss, or high gloss, remember that the higher the sheen, the harder it is to apply the paint. High-gloss paint requires much better surface preparation before painting to decrease imperfections, but it does result in a higher-end look.

WALLS AND CEILINGS

We are very adamant about using *flat* paint on walls and ceilings. We say this knowing that anyone reading this with children at home just rolled their eyes at us. As we have already mentioned, ask any paint clerk what sheen to choose for walls, and nine out of ten times, they'll respond with eggshell. This level of sheen is thought to be easier to clean and is undeniably popular with, well, everyone.

The reason we don't consider eggshell to be an option for walls is because any amount of sheen on the wall enhances its imperfections. Flat paint has the least amount of reflection, which means that your chosen color will appear deeper and richer. No one has perfect walls, and flat paint smooths out those imperfections beautifully. And while we don't have kids at home, we've never had an issue cleaning our walls. Bonus: Flat paint is the easiest to repair, because you can't see the touch up!

If you want to see us have a heart attack, show us a video of someone painting an accent wall in a dark-colored, high-sheen paint. Our deepest condolences to your walls.

TRIM AND CABINETRY

Historically, trim and cabinetry were often painted with a high-sheen oil-based paint, which works well on high-traffic and high-touch surfaces because it dries hard and is resistant to scuffing. The main drawback of oil-based paint is that it tends to be high in volatile organic compounds (VOCs), introducing environmental and health risks into your space. Additionally, oil-based paints tend to yellow and crack with time. Modern trim and cabinetry paints are water-based and lower in VOCs. These new hybrid paints will sport words like *urethane*, *alkyd*, and *enamel*—and they have superior hardening power while still remaining flexible. These paints will not yellow over time and are less prone to cracking.

Visually, the higher-sheen paint elevates your millwork and helps to distinguish it from the walls. The paint's ability to reflect light also makes it ideal for enhancing the architectural details in your home.

For items with more detail—like door casings, baseboard, and crown molding—we tend to paint in semi-gloss. For surfaces that are larger or have less detail, like wall paneling or cabinets, we are more likely to choose satin. These are just preferences, however, not rules, and such preferences can change depending on the look you are trying to achieve.

There's More to Color than Paint

Throughout this chapter, we've talked about color in the context of paint. But color lives everywhere in a home, not just on the walls. It's woven through textures, materials, patterns, and light itself. Once you start to see color as more than just paint, your palette expands dramatically.

WALLPAPER

Wallpaper has a storied history. It was used in Georgian and Victorian homes to bring pattern and luxury to rooms beyond the architectural detail alone. Within our lifetimes, wallpaper has gone from "very on trend" (think early '90s kitchen cows) to "very off trend" (early 2000s), and now . . .

it's back! We would argue that wallpaper is timeless, but check in with us again in ten or twenty years, and we'll see if we feel the same way.

Regardless, wallpaper offers an opportunity to add texture and personality to a space in a way that paint simply cannot. This works especially well as a moment of surprise in a small or transitional space—such as a vestibule, powder room, or bedroom.

When selecting wallpaper, consider the following:

+ Scale: Large patterns tend to make a statement, while smaller or tonal patterns act more as a background texture.

+ Palette: Coordinate the background or base colors in the wallpaper with the trim and furnishings in the room for a more cohesive look. You can bring a wallpaper sample to the paint store for color matching.

+ Texture: Beyond pattern or color, there is an opportunity to add texture with grass-cloth, woven, or other natural wallpapers.

As for installing wallpaper—this is a mixed bag. In the beginning of our renovation journey, we hired a professional for application, as the rooms were more complex, the paper was expensive, and we couldn't afford to make a mistake. But in the Maine cabin, we took a leap of faith and did it ourselves. It was challenging at first, but we got the hang of it, and despite the odds, we are still married, and happily so!

LEFT: We chose a busy wallpaper for our closets to help break up the otherwise-neutral bedroom and bathroom. We love how the paper looks like camouflage even though the print actually shows cows and barns.

RIGHT: In the first version of the Maine cabin guest room, Stephen hand-painted a plaid mural. When it came time to redo the room, we wanted to elevate it with a more sophisticated paper.

SPECIALTY FINISHES

There are other options if you are looking to add more depth to your space, like limewash and Roman Clay, which are paint-application techniques that result in a finish full of movement and depth. The imperfection of the hand-applied process also adds so much character.

+ Limewash: a mineral-based paint that dries with a soft, cloudy variation, adding additional depth without adding shine

+ Roman Clay: a plaster-like finish with a velvety texture and subtle shifts in tone and sheen

We first used Roman Clay in our Boston Victorian primary suite. We knew we wanted the walls to be white, but we didn't want them to feel, well, basic. We applied Roman Clay, and the result has so much depth. You can see variance in the sheen when the light reflects off the surface, and when you run your hand along the wall, it feels as smooth as glass. The finish *feels* luxurious. We even completed the entire application in a singlc day! Big fans.

TEXTILES AND UPHOLSTERY

Fabric is the most forgiving and flexible way to layer more color into your whole-home color palette. Maybe you like to keep things more neutral on the walls—and really go wild with textiles. If so, curtains, rugs, and furniture present the perfect opportunities to add warmth, texture, and variation to your space.

LEFT: White walls gave us the opportunity to work with more saturated furnishings, like this big green sofa and an orange patterned rug in the Maine cabin living room.

RIGHT: We sourced red corduroy bench cushions that made David nostalgic for the interior of his grandparents' 1986 Buick LeSabre.

ART AND DÉCOR

Often it's the finishing touches that bring personality and energy to a space. Art, in particular, can completely shift how a room feels. You can incorporate it in one of two ways (or a little bit of both!).

Selecting art after finalizing wall colors allows you to look for pieces that complement the space rather than compete with it. Alternatively, you can use art as the color inspiration around which to build your palette.

The same rule applies to décor: Ceramics, books, plants, etc., offer the ability to weave color into your space, giving the room's palette a sense of balance.

QUESTIONS TO CONSIDER

Before you pick up a paint brush, here are some questions
you might want to consider as you select colors:

What is the light like in your space?

Spend time observing how light behaves in your home. Notice how
the same wall shifts in tone throughout the day. Pay attention to
where natural light pours in, and where artificial light takes over.
What direction do the windows face? How might this room shift
with the seasons? Taking a few days to live with swatches taped on
different walls can reveal more than any fan deck ever could.

What is the feeling you are trying to evoke?

Color is as emotional as it is subjective, and it's worth asking
yourself how you want a room to *feel*. Do you want calm and
spaciousness, or intimacy and focus? A deep, saturated hue can
create a sense of enclosure that feels cozy and grounded, while
lighter tones can open up a space and make it feel airy. Don't worry
about color trends—think about how you want to use the space and
what color choices might help support that.

How can you incorporate color in other ways?

Color doesn't have to stop at the walls. Extending a hue onto the
ceiling or trim can make a space feel elevated and immersive. You
can add depth and texture to the space with a specialty finish or
a patterned wallpaper, or go bold with art and décor. The key is to
think holistically about how color wraps the room, defining both
mood and materiality.

SALVAGE & THRIFT

Whenever we give someone a tour of our home, we always tell the same stories. "Oh, we found that a few years ago during a trip to Brimfield," or "We restored that piece and it took us months." The most interesting parts of our home are the pieces that carry history, even if they aren't original to the house. This chapter explores how to bring that sense of history into your own space through reclaimed materials, thrifted objects, and architectural finds. We'll share where to look, what to look for, and how to transform forgotten items into design features.

Patina

Who is she, and why do we love her?

"Patina" typically refers to the discoloration or wear that develops on natural surfaces like metal, leather, and wood over time from normal use or exposure to the elements. The Statue of Liberty is a great example of patina—the green color, also called "verdigris," forms when copper is exposed to oxygen and the environment over time. Whether made by nature or by humans, the patina of an object tells a unique story of its history and use.

For interiors, we think of patina more romantically: the worn butcher-block table with grooves from years of meal preparation; pine floors with wear marks formed by muddy boots and your excited family pet; mantelpieces pocked with nail holes where the stockings are hung each Christmas. These are the things that remind us a home is lived in and loved—the collection of experiences that contribute to the character of a home.

Whether you inherit patina or created it yourself over time, we encourage you to lean into these imperfections. Further, using natural finishes that wear with time—like wood, brass, or marble—is a sure way to layer plenty of character into your own home, no matter the age.

Patina comes in all shapes and sizes. Layering items of different ages and eras can make your space feel uniquely you.

Prioritizing Salvaged Pieces

If patina can develop only with time, how can we insert patina into a new home or design? Well, you're in luck, because salvaged items can be found almost anywhere—and finding them is the most fun part of the process. Some of our all-time favorite pieces were found on the side of the road, the happenstance of the discovery making them even more magical. Here are a few places to look during your hunt for amazing items:

ANTIQUE SHOPS

This isn't groundbreaking information, but antique shops are the most approachable place to start. Antique shops come in all shapes and sizes, depending on who has curated them. Some focus more on jewelry, some art, some on early American furniture. They can get pretty niche. We tend to gravitate toward antique malls, where you'll find a large variety of items all in one place. Our best advice is to visit as many antique shops as you can. It makes for a fabulous weekend activity, and the more you do it, the likelier you are to find incredible pieces.

THRIFT SHOPS AND YARD SALES

If antique shops are curated experiences, thrift shops and yard sales are the Wild West. Sure, you'll have to sort through other people's "junk," but there are still so many treasures to be discovered. Take the Goodwill art section, for example—a true hodgepodge of styles and sensibilities—but so fun to sort through. For only three bucks, you can find a really cool art piece in a terrible frame or, just as likely, the worst art you have ever seen in a beautiful frame. It's the mixing and matching that has allowed us to create charming gallery walls as focal points in some of our favorite rooms.

ARCHITECTURAL SALVAGE

While antique shops generally focus on décor, furniture, and knickknacks, architectural salvage shops carry all the things typically affixed to a home. We're talking old windows, doors, mantelpieces, reclaimed lumber, flooring, plumbing and light fixtures—the list goes on. The saints that own these shops step in when historical buildings are being demolished or renovated and, to our benefit, put them up for sale! This can be a great resource not only for finding items that your house might be missing (like that random old doorknob), but also for finding beautiful pieces that can inspire an entire room.

Every piece on this gallery wall was found from either a yard sale, a thrift shop, or a local artist. None of the pieces are particularly special, but together they mean something special to us.

NOR'EAST ARCHITECTURAL ANTIQUES
ENTRANCE

LEFT: Documenting our many visits to Nor'East Architectural Antiques, one of our favorite local salvage locations.

ABOVE: You may recognize this antique milk-glass pendant light in just a couple of pages.

Incorporating Salvaged Items

Salvaged items have played a key role in making our Boston Victorian feel authentic to its age. Some items we thrifted, some we salvaged, and some we found in the basement of the house itself. Weaving these pieces through our home has proven to be the most enjoyable and impactful aspect of our renovation journey.

SMALL CURIOSITIES

Sometimes the smallest items can make the biggest impact. We are always on the lookout for things like brass doorknobs or faceplates, which, with a little polishing, shine right up. This is an inexpensive way to make a big impact and add character to a space. We include small light fixtures or lanterns in this group, too—salvaged versions always preferred over modern store-bought options. This commitment to hardware feels innately different from furniture or décor, because when installed, they literally become part of the home.

PIECES LEFT BEHIND

After we closed on the Boston Victorian, we started the process of sorting through what the previous owner had left behind. While much of the original trim and detail had been stripped from the walls, we did find a pile of "stuff" in the basement, among which were bits and pieces of door trims or casings, scraps of crown molding, and a couple of bigger items that made us squeal.

OUR LIVING ROOM MANTELPIECE

The largest item left behind was a fully intact mantelpiece. It was covered in grime, but a bit of cleaning revealed a beautiful amber color. The detailing correlated with the mantel in the entryway, but there was no obvious home for this piece, which begged the question: How did it get here? We dug through old real-estate photos and found that a fireplace and chimney had been removed from the center of the home—which explained the huge pile of bricks we also discovered in the basement. Once we pieced the clues together, there wasn't even a question: The mantel would need to be added back to the home.

We ended up doing a lot more than just putting the mantel back. We changed the entire design of the room to accommodate it. We framed in a modern gas fireplace on an exterior wall, creating a bump-out and a new focal point. Ghosted outlines on the mantel's edge provided us with a blueprint for the room's baseboard and chair-rail size and placement.

Years later, we had lunch with the couple who had owned the house in the 1970s and 1980s. We gave them a tour of the house, and we were a nervous wreck. "We swear we weren't the ones who gutted it!" But those nerves were quickly put to ease as we entered the living room. "You saved the mantel!" one of the previous owners said. "I stripped the paint from it for weeks while I was pregnant with our first child." Immediately, all the effort to resurrect the piece paid off. The mantel itself is beautiful, but it's the story that gives it even more character.

We decided to frame out a new fireplace just days before plaster was scheduled. It's hard to imagine this room without its original mantel and the structure and symmetry that it provides.

A very similar story can be told about our favorite spot in the Boston Victorian kitchen: the pantry. Within that same pile of stuff, there were two glass doors as well as the frame they sat in. We turned again to old real estate photos and found that they were the original kitchen-pantry doors. So when we started to design our kitchen the second time, we knew the original pantry would become the main feature. We removed the original shellac with denatured alcohol and steel wool, then applied a fresh coat that will carry these doors through the next hundred years.

LEFT: The most important pile of wood we have ever found. Here, you can see the mantel that now lives in the Boston Victorian living room.

RIGHT: After being restored and with careful planning, the pantry doors were returned to the Boston kitchen.

THE TRIM LIVES ON

The major focal point of our Boston Victorian parlor design is the custom built-in that separates it from the dining room. We spent hours mocking up the design digitally, and we worked closely with a local cabinetmaker to bring our vision to life. One day, while reviewing our design, we had an epiphany. "We should use the trim in the basement!" Once again, we returned to the aforementioned pile of stuff and fished out remnants of the old door and window casings. With just enough remaining to serve as the vertical faces of the built-in, we cleaned up the trim and incorporated it into the plan. It was perfect. Adding this detail, which still exists in the adjacent entry, makes the built-in feel as if it has always been there.

Our tool kit for sprucing up found pieces includes:

+ Restore-A-Finish: Worked with some 0000-steel wool (pronounced "quad zero" steel wool) and a rag, this product can immediately bring dull pieces to new life without stripping.

+ Brasso or Bar Keepers Friend: These products clean and polish metals back to their original glow. We love patina, but sometimes a piece covered in grime or paint can do with a reset.

+ Crockpot: A dedicated crockpot is the perfect way to remove paint from old hardware. We typically just use water and dish soap (you can use vinegar, too) and let it sit. After a few hours, steel wool or a soft wire brush is all you'll need.

OPPOSITE: In most cases, we are not in favor of painting original woodwork, but we think the exception makes sense here.

Our Approach in the Maine Cabin

The Maine cabin has forced us to consider salvage in a different capacity. Every decision in the Boston Victorian was additive; starting from nothing, we actively looked for ways to insert character back into the home. In contrast, our Maine cabin was built in 1975 and was lived in by the same family for the following fifty years. With that home, we inherited all kinds of original details—like wood paneling and wide-plank pine floors. We also inherited things that needed updating, like carpeted bedrooms, dated bathrooms, and a worn-down kitchen. As we took stock of the home, we asked ourselves a new set of questions: *What here contributes to character? And what gets removed?*

When it came time to design our primary suite, we found ourselves laboring over the elephant in the room: the rough-sawn paneling. Hanging over our heads, it was dark and felt oppressive. On the other hand, it was unique and contributed so much to why we call this house a *cabin*. In other words, it had character built in.

The solution was to embrace the material by making it a primary feature of the room, but in a new way. We picked a panel height and, with the use of a track saw, removed all the wood paneling above it. The removed material was repurposed to make the feature continuous throughout the entire room. We then added new trim to cap the paneling and installed a new baseboard. It was intensive in time and labor, but we found a way to retain the character while elevating the entire space.

As we continue our Maine cabin renovation, we are always looking for opportunities to elevate the existing materials or use vintage pieces that defined the era.

Old Pieces, New Life

Every salvaged piece carries a story in its patina, a history written into the material that lives on within our home. For us, salvage isn't about nostalgia for what's old. It's about weaving history into the present, giving your space an authenticity that can't be replicated. When you bring salvaged pieces into your home, you aren't just decorating—you're layering the story, honoring the character, and allowing your design to become part of a much longer conversation.

So, yeah, pick up that weird thing on the side of the road and figure out how you can use it in your home!

LEFT: The original Maine cabin primary suite felt quite dark. With a little rearranging of the wood paneling, we made the space feel more cohesive. Also, the wide-plank wood floors are to die for.

QUESTIONS TO CONSIDER

Whether you have a new or old house, salvaged items are a great way to insert character into your home. When searching for salvaged pieces, consider the following questions:

What existing details could you keep, repair, or spotlight instead of replacing?

Does your home have details you already love or that you could grow to love? As you approach a space, take stock of what already exists in it. If you reframe a detail or flaw as an asset, how might that affect your design?

Does that thing you're looking for need to be new?

Consider searching for second-hand pieces before shopping for new. Beyond the antique and thrift shops, online resources like Marketplace are a great place to find items within your community. Pre-loved items will have innate character, and you'll likely save some money (and the environment!) in the process.

Can you salvage from your own house?

You may not have inherited a basement full of old parts like we did, but does your house have details you love? If you're doing any demo, consider whether those items can be celebrated or repurposed elsewhere.

FURNISHING & DÉCOR

If architecture gives your home its framework, furnishings and décor give it life. Each piece adds another layer of personality, and this chapter explores how to select pieces that feel intentional and collected rather than over-styled to perfection. We'll talk about mixing styles, honoring personal history, and creating moments that invite conversation. Whether you're designing from scratch or rearranging what you already own, this chapter is about creating spaces you love because they mean something to you.

A Story of Things

Every object tells a story; the key is giving it a place to speak.

In 1933, at the height of the Depression and at the age of 16, Elsie went to work for Cities Service (today's Citgo). Elsie was often the breadwinner for the family, and from her pay, she was allowed 15 cents a day—five for the trolley, five for lunch, and five to pocket. One day, a clock in a store window caught her eye. She had recently gotten a small pay raise and wisely kept this news from her mother. She bought the clock on layaway and worked until it was finally hers.

We don't know how she hid this from her family or how she explained the clock's appearance after she paid it off. But the clock stayed with her in her first home in Everett, Massachusetts, then through years in Michigan, and back to Boston again.

Every Sunday before Mass, Elsie's husband, Lawrence, would wind up the clock for the week ahead. The small enclosure on the bottom served as a secret spot to store tickets, notes, and other things you absolutely could not lose.

After Elsie and Lawrence passed, the clock spent years in storage until my father offered it to me, along with this story. Today it hangs in our parlor, a simple, steadfast symbol of resilience and devotion. I miss you, Nana. Thank you for the gift.

Love,

Stephen

ABOVE: The clock works like a charm, but we keep it unwound. Chiming every half hour is crazy.

LEFT: When Stephen inherited his Nana's clock, we knew that we wanted to celebrate it. So, when laying out our parlor molding, we made sure that the proportions framed it perfectly.

Finding and Celebrating Stories

It's easy to understand why family heirlooms have innate character. Heirlooms come with a generational game of telephone that forms the pieces of their story. And the story is what makes them special. Sure, we think Stephen's grandmother's clock is beautiful, but we can't say we would have bought it if we'd passed it in a thrift shop. The context is what we love so much about it, and when someone visits our Boston Victorian parlor, it's the story we tell.

Now, not all your home furnishings can be heirlooms—that would be impossible. But if you look around, I'm sure you'll find a story in a lot of your favorite items. The story might be how you found it, where you found it, or who you were with when it came into your possession. It may be something you loved as a child or that you collected over the years.

When we finished renovating a guestroom in our Maine cabin, something didn't quite feel right. We had followed all our rules: added millwork to match the house, layered in paneling for texture, picked a color that fit our whole-home palette, and even used vintage-inspired furnishings. And yet, it still felt *too* new.

The answer was in our growing collection of vintage paint-by-numbers. The reason we love them? Stephen loves that they tell a story. Not the literal story of the subject matter, but of the people who painted them. Were they kids? Adults? Earnest attempts at art or simply filling an afternoon? That mystery is part of their magic. David loves the stories of where and how we found them—hanging on the wall of a deli or discovered in a late-night bidding war on eBay. Once we hung a gallery wall of them, the room came alive. Suddenly, the space had a point of view—playful, imperfect, iconically tacky.

Furnishing with Intention

Furniture is the part of home design we interact with most. It defines how you live in a space—where you eat, work, gather, and enjoy your morning coffee. The pieces you choose have a direct impact on how you move through your day and through your home. It might sound like we're giving furniture too much credit, but think about it—where are you reading this book right now? (We hope you're comfortable!)

When we think about what gives furniture character, there is more than just age, patina, and color to consider. With furniture, we must also contemplate what makes it unique or interesting—its form, material, or function. Think about not only each individual piece but also how they work together as a collection. The relationship between these pieces is where a home's personality often takes shape.

START WITH THE ANCHORS

Every room has its anchor piece—it might be a sofa, the dining table, or the bed—that sets the proportion and mood for the space. Consider it an opportunity to showcase something special. In our Maine cabin living room, the green sofa became that anchor piece, helping to dictate

Despite our fascination with paint-by-numbers, we have yet to complete one ourselves.

Architects on Architecture

everything else in the room: the palette, the rug size and color, even the lamp heights. While we purchased the sofa new, we spent months searching for something that felt both unique and true to the space. The dark-green corduroy feels appropriate for the era of the house, and its modularity allowed us to wrap it around the perimeter of the room—giving it a bespoke, built-in look.

DON'T LET "STYLE" BE A BOX

When we share photos of our Boston Victorian home online, we're often asked: "What do you call this style?" We're always tempted to answer: "Idk . . . ours."

What people usually want are keywords, a label they can use to search for similar ideas. The truth is, we don't really have a neat definition. Our approach has evolved naturally over time by listening to the house for architectural cues while furnishing it with pieces we love. Look at any room in our Boston Victorian and you'll see two constants: a built-in that nods to the home's history and furnishings that lean more midcentury. Something fussy paired with something sleek.

In the Maine cabin, we're choosing pieces based on a slightly different set of criteria, always looking for pieces that are appropriate for a cabin but with a retro flair. This balancing act is why this project has taken on such a new vibe from those we have completed previously.

We'd like to say that we always have a grand plan, but honestly, each home style was an evolution that came with time. All to say, style doesn't need to be a fixed set of rules.

Architecture might ask for respect, but furnishings give you freedom. We think it's the flirtation between styles that makes a space feel layered and personal.

MATERIAL MATTERS

In the way we've spoken about the beauty of patina in architectural detail, the same can be said for furniture. Natural materials age gracefully; synthetic ones only age. When we're sourcing furniture, we typically opt for woods, metals, stone, or leather that will develop a patina. A marble tabletop etched from use feels like a diary. A leather chair scuffed at the arms becomes more inviting, not less. These surfaces don't reject time—they record it—and become even better with age.

SCALE AND ZONING

Furniture should feel in proportion not only to the room but also to the architecture itself. High ceilings and tall windows can support larger, heavier pieces, while smaller rooms benefit from petite furniture that lifts off the floor, giving the space more room to breathe. Think of furniture as a part of the architectural composition—it shapes how a room is perceived, not just how it's used.

When assessing scale, look beyond dimensions. Pay attention to visual weight—the way a piece feels in a space. A slender-legged chair may occupy the same footprint as a club chair yet appear lighter because it allows light to pass through it.

In larger spaces, you can use furniture to define zones for different activities. Floating a couch in the middle of a room can define a seating area, and rugs can break up an otherwise open floor plan. In smaller rooms, furniture can carve out moments of purpose—a reading chair in a sunny corner, a bench by the entry, or a desk tucked behind a sofa. Thoughtful zoning makes a space feel intentional and maximizes every square foot.

THE HUNT AND THE EDIT

Throughout our adult lives, like many people, we've moved multiple times. And with each move, the scale of our homes—and the furniture that fits them—has changed. We went from separate apartments to our first shared one-bedroom, then to our first home, then back to a small apartment, and eventually to our Boston Victorian. With every move came the same questions:

"Do we really want to move this flat-pack dresser again?"
"This couch is so worn in, but I love it."
"How are we going to furnish three bedrooms?"

Our favorite furniture wasn't bought in a weekend. It was found over time—at estate sales, at flea markets, on Marketplace, or from local craftspeople whose work we admire. We keep search alerts for specific pieces ("vintage record cabinet," "round oak dining table," etc.) and wait for the right one to appear. The long game merely builds character.

In the meantime, live with what you have. Rearrange, experiment, and pay attention to what works and what doesn't. Use placeholders until you find the right fit or can afford to upgrade. Sometimes, living without something teaches you exactly what you want.

Furnishing with intention means slowing down, trusting your instincts, and allowing time to reveal what truly fits. Furniture is more than what fills a space—it's how you experience it. When chosen with care and patience, the pieces you live with every day become quiet reflections of who you are and how you live.

Décor Is Your Story

Where furniture defines how you live, décor reveals who you are. It's the layer that brings emotion and personality into the space, the part that turns rooms from "designed" to "lived in." When we think about character through the lens of décor, it's not about the age or quality but rather about looking around a room and evoking curiosity.

Here's a thought experiment: If a total stranger walked into your living room on their own, would they get a sense of the person who lives there?

START WITH MEANINGFUL OBJECTS

Your home should be weirder. That doesn't (necessarily) mean cluttered or chaotic—it means personal, imperfect, and a little unexpected. The most interesting rooms are the ones that make you pause and ask, "What's the story here?"

Build vignettes around items with stories—family mementos, travel finds, or handmade pieces. These objects

The Boston entry has undergone a few iterations over the years. Here you can see David's beloved light fixture, which he called "the Steel Magnolia." Others called it "a Dementor coming out of the ceiling."

may not "match," but they make the space feel like it belongs to someone real. In our homes, the things that make us smile are rarely the perfect ones. A hand-carved duck from the cutest old man at the craft fair or the gold statue of a flamingo found on the dance floor (both real examples). The things you choose to display are a quiet biography—evidence of where you've been or something only you have experienced.

SHOW OFF YOUR COLLECTION

One surefire way to insert personality into a room is by integrating a favorite collection. Whether it's inherited china displayed in the dining room or an entire gallery wall of silhouette portraits (or paint-by-numbers!), collections reveal your quirks and curiosities.

If that sounds too maximalist for your taste, think smaller. A collection doesn't have to dominate a room—it can simply serve as a pleasant surprise. In our Maine cabin living room, there's a small grass-cloth box that we keep on the coffee table. Most of the time, it remains closed, binoculars perched on top—but open it and a treasure is revealed: Stephen's childhood rock collection. Something that was once in the back of a closet is now proudly displayed for a guest to discover. Collections, large or small, make rooms feel like extensions of their owners.

Stephen's childhood rock collection is out for display at the Maine cabin. Not pictured (or allowed): David's Pokémon card collection.

LIVING DÉCOR, THE POWER OF PLANTS

If your home ever feels stale, add something that *lives*. Plants soften architectural edges and introduce organic forms that make rooms feel more alive—literally. They're natural sculptures that introduce vibrancy, and a little bit of chaos.

We're pretty sure every room in our home has some kind of plant. A large ficus can give an empty corner new life. Smaller plants grouped on a windowsill or layered on a shelf add texture and a sense of movement.

The best part? Plants reward care with growth. Unlike most décor, they evolve with you—stretching toward the light, taking up space, reminding you that homes, like people, are living things.

STYLING, NOT STAGING

Styling is tricky. There are no real "rules," and much of it comes down to personal taste. But there are a few guidelines that can help:

+ Vary height and scale so your eyes move through the space naturally.
+ Pay attention to negative space—gaps are what give the things you love room to speak.
+ Mix colors and textures to create depth and warmth.
+ Use décor to echo your room's palette at a smaller scale, distributing color evenly throughout the space.

You'll notice none of these guidelines dictate what to style with—that's entirely up to you. Don't be afraid to move things around. We change vignettes constantly, rotating objects from one room to another. It keeps the house feeling fresh without buying anything new. Styling is as much about evolution as it is about placement.

Perfection, however, is the enemy. A candle half burned, a throw draped imperfectly, or a book left open are all small reminders that this is a home in use, and not a showroom.

Lighting

We are sticklers for good lighting and will fuss over options for hours. Often approached as an afterthought, artificial light is a design element that changes everything. It defines how we see color, how we experience texture, and how we feel in a room.

LAYERS OF LIGHT

Good lighting works in layers.

Start with **ambient lighting**, the general illumination that fills the room. This can come from ceiling fixtures, recessed can lights, or brighter floor and table lamps. We primarily rely on the latter, preferring the glow of a lamp to the glare of overhead fixtures. The "big lights" are reserved strictly for cooking and cleaning.

Next is **task lighting**—focused light placed intentionally for reading, cooking, grooming, or working. Think table lamps, bedside sconces, desk lamps, and vanity lights.

Finally, there's **accent lighting**, the jewelry of a room. It's used to highlight something specific: a picture light illuminating artwork, sconces flanking a mirror, or directional lighting to emphasize architectural detail. Alternatively, accent lighting can be the art itself—small decorative lamps that exist purely for charm or novelty.

Each layer serves a different purpose, but it's the combination of all three that creates atmosphere. A single overhead light can make a space feel like an interrogation room, whereas multiple light sources placed at varying heights can make a space feel warm, dimensional, and alive.

RIGHT, BOTTOM: If you ever visit our house, ask Alexa to turn on Rihanna. She shines bright like a diamond.

Light color, referred to as temperature, dramatically affects how your home feels. Light temperature is measured in kelvins (K). Warm light (2500 K–3000 K) creates comfort and intimacy, while cooler light (3500 K and above) feels more like daylight (or a hospital).

We'd love to tell you that *any* color temperature can give your home character, but we just don't believe that's true. Humans evolved by firelight, and our homes were once lit by candles and gas lamps. Warm light is always the answer. We use slightly cooler temperatures only for functional spaces, like kitchens or bathrooms, where clarity is key.

Once measured in watts (how much energy an incandescent bulb used), brightness is now measured universally in lumens. For reference, here's a quick comparison between the two units of measurement:

- 40 watts = 450 lumens
- 60 watts = 800 lumens
- 100 watts = 1600 lumens

Matching color temperatures across a room keeps light cohesive and helps your eyes adjust more comfortably. It's a subtle detail, but one that can make your home feel calmer, more intentional, and beautifully lit.

	Temperature (Kelvins)	Brightness (Lumens)
Living Spaces (Bedrooms, Living Rooms, Offices)	2500–2700 K	450–800 lumens
Functional Spaces (Kitchens, Bathrooms)	Up to 3000 K	Up to 1100 lumens

Bringing It All Together

Furniture shapes how you live, décor shows who you are, and lighting reveals it all. Together, they form the language of your home—structure, soul, and atmosphere. They remind us that character doesn't come from perfection but from layers—the ones we inherit, the ones we build, and the ones that grow with us.

QUESTIONS TO CONSIDER

It's important to remember that how you choose to furnish and decorate your home is fully up to you, not anyone else. Here are some questions to help challenge you in the process:

How do you want to live in your space?

Before thinking about aesthetics, consider the room's function. Where do you naturally gather? How do you like to start and end your day? Does your current furniture support those routines? Let those answers guide how you furnish. The most character-filled rooms are ones that work beautifully for how you actually live.

What stories do your objects tell?

Look around at the things you've chosen to keep. Do they showcase who you are, or do they just take up space? Which objects have meaning, history, or personality? Are there small changes you can make to celebrate them? Sometimes, a single sentimental piece says more than an entire shelf of décor.

Does your space feel like you?

Or does it feel like the Target home section? Every decision, from the furniture you invest in to the lamp you turn on before bed, contributes to your home's personality. Ask yourself what moments make you happiest and whether your surroundings support those moments. The goal isn't merely to decorate; it's to create a place that makes you happy. *That's* what gives it character.

A little dinner get-together with our friends, Laura and Ben; our editor, Alex; and our lifestyle photographer, Coy. Thank you, Coy, for so many of the beautiful images in this book, and for deleting the photos of us eating before we ever saw them.

Good Character Takes Time

This is a lesson we've only started to understand:
Your home gets better with time.

As we design new spaces, we try to think of them holistically and completely, and we hope to love them when they are done.

But there is something special that only happens with time. You swap out the rug for the perfect vintage piece, or you gradually add items that tell a story. The brand-new counters start to etch and bruise, and the floors begin to show scratches from the dog's routine. The room becomes loved and lived in.

We wrote this book to help define what character is and how you can incorporate it into your own home. We've told our stories and passed on our lessons, and we really hope you have taken away some inspiration. We truly believe there is a lot you can do to add craft and intention right from the start. What we really want to instill is the idea that, sometimes, the best thing you can do is live in and learn from your spaces. In an age where so much of what we seek is instant gratification, let your home evolve gracefully.

Design your spaces to love them. Live in your spaces to cherish them.

PART TWO
The
Rooms

BOSTON VICTORIAN

Built in 1893, this 2,400-square-foot Victorian home is exemplary of the Queen Anne style. Located in Boston's largest neighborhood of Dorchester, this home is a small piece of a vibrant and loving community. This project is responsible for who we are today, and our proudest accomplishment.

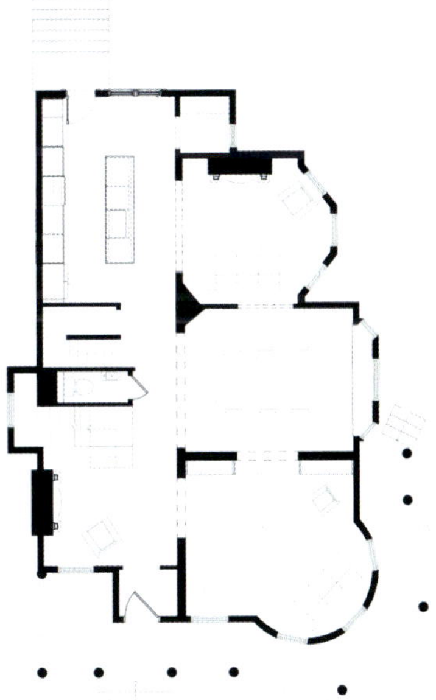

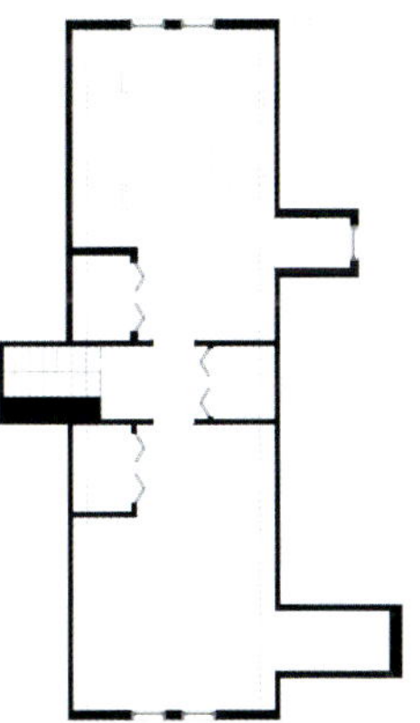

The woodwork in the entry was one of the few things spared when the home was gutted by a previous owner. The fireplace tile surround was an unexpected find, hidden behind an old brass insert.

ABOVE: We would be remiss not to mention Stephen's mother, Nancy. She is an avid thrifter with a great eye, and you can find many of her discoveries throughout this room and the rest of our home.

RIGHT: Somewhere along the way, David discovered the work of Pat Cantin, a painter from Montreal, and won this piece at auction. The pink works so well in this sea of green.

OPPOSITE: This perspective of the parlor is one of our favorites.

ABOVE: The small moments in any space are an opportunity to tell a story: the balsa wood house model from Stephen's college days; the small cutting board we received as a wedding gift; the photo book from our honeymoon in Europe; and even the piano that neither of us know how to play.

ABOVE: We were once invited to lunch by our neighbors, who have lived in this neighborhood for decades. There, they introduced us to the couple that owned our home in the 1970s, who presented us with a gift—a sketch of our home that they have held onto for all these years. Stephen cried as he unwrapped the framed image that now hangs above the piano.

ABOVE: We can't resist fresh flowers on the dining room table. Tulips in spring, sunflowers in summer, and hydrangeas from the yard in fall.

Since it sits at the center of the home, we decided early on to create a dining room we actually use, whether it's just us or a group of friends. Light and bright, it provides a relief from the bold parlor and the living room beyond.

ABOVE: The half bath, affectionately referred to as "the Harry Potter bathroom," is nestled into the space where a coat closet once was. Our friend, Josh Linder, deserves the credit for this brilliant idea and for encouraging us to go bold from the very beginning.

Not the caption you may expect, but we want to talk about the best ceiling height: nine feet. For this kitchen, the three-foot-tall island, the three-foot space between the island and pendant, and the three-foot pendant feels like the perfect ratio.

FAQ: The range hood is hidden in the cabinet above it. And yes, we need a ladder to reach those upper-upper cabinets!

LEFT: One of our favorite features of
this kitchen is its connection to the
backyard. Hosting friends and family in
the warmer months feels magical.

The goal for the pantry was to be
beautiful and functional. The original
pantry doors with their wavy glass
inspired the entire design, and we love
how it feels as if it's always been here.

The cased opening between these two spaces helps define each as their own, all while maintaining an intimate connection.

A television over the fireplace is controversial at best, but in a home full of windows, we had few options. When backed into a corner like this one, a TV disguised as art is a great option. We have spent countless evenings in this exact spot and really appreciate the convenience of the nearby kitchen.

Would you have painted the inside of the cased opening the same color as the kitchen, as we did? Or would you have painted it the same color as the living room as we did at first, only to change it?

Vignettes that we particularly love. The
sun pouring in, a collection of hand-drawn
honeybees, and the connection between spaces.

When designing the primary
suite, we wanted to keep
things neutral, creating a
calming effect of a light and
bright space to start and
end each day.

We renovated this entire suite over a six-week period. At the end, exhausted and in need of art, we took turns creating continuous line portraits of each other, blindfolded (right). We will let you guess who is who.

ABOVE: A week after meeting his college roommate, Peter, Stephen was asked a series of interview questions. In return, Peter drew a pair of high-heeled shoes that best represented Stephen's responses. Thank you, Peter.

RIGHT: These freestanding elevator doors were salvaged from a hotel in Boston. We initially hoped to hang them, but quickly abandoned the idea when we realized how impractical that would be. They are now the heaviest décor that we own.

ABOVE: Someone once referred to our shower as "the Lincoln Memorial." It is one of our proudest accomplishments.

This guest bedroom is light and bright and a great example of how much antique pieces (and plants) can add to a space. The vintage rug and brass lamp are among our favorite finds.

We created "the Princess Peak" by removing
a couple of non-supporting joists to give this
ceiling its unique shape. We added an ornate
wood piece above the window to give the
space a bit of flair.

RIGHT: Passing by with guests, a messy bed
reminds you why these spaces exist.

We renovated our third floor/attic seven years after living in the home. Here, the goal was to create a light, bright, and functional space. This side serves as "the snug" where we hang out at the end of the day and watch TV.

For years we worked from home with computers and monitors piled up on the dining room table. Creating a dedicated office space completely transformed how we move through our day and experience our own home.

In short, if you were looking for a sign to convert a space into something more functional, this is it!

In classic Victorian style, our home has many small dormers. When renovating, we wanted to use every nook and cranny in an interesting or thoughtful way.

This beauty is filled with imperfection. The exterior has seen repairs over the years, but many of the 133-year-old materials still exist. Someday we will have saved enough money to give her the attention she deserves.

Our home is situated on a busy corner lot in a dense
neighborhood. Since the beginning, we have thought of ways
to make our little outdoor space an oasis in the city. In the
back, we added a sunken pea-stone patio and a large fence
for more privacy. In the front yard, we opted for a baluster
fence, allowing for better connection with neighbors and
views of the garden from the sidewalk.

MAINE CABIN

Built in 1975, this 1,500-square-foot chalet-style home was loved by a single family for over fifty years. Perched on a tidal river in Midcoast Maine, this home is surrounded by natural beauty. Here we were introduced to a way of life and community that we have grown to love.

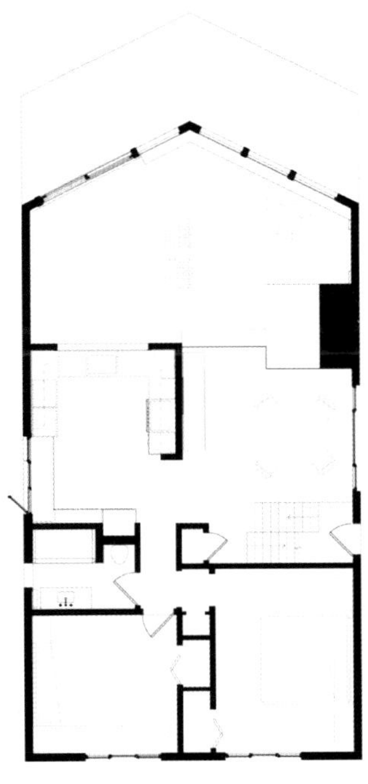

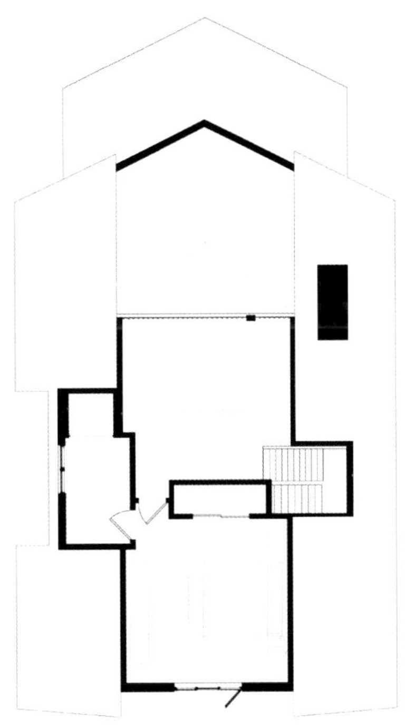

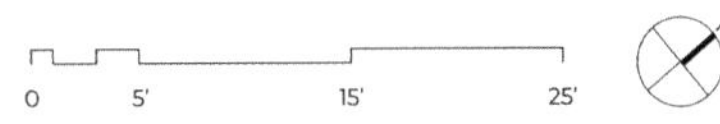

This is the space where we spend most of our time these days. It is where we wrote this book and this caption. By the evening, the lamps are turned on, the taper candles are lit, and we begin to wind down.

The greatest feature of this home is
one we cannot take any credit for—its
connection to the outdoors.

These are the views we recall in the dead of Maine winter. Spring will eventually come, and it will be green.

ABOVE, RIGHT: Made of local stone, the fireplace is the heart of the first floor. Evening fires warm the living room, dining room, and loft above during the fall and winter months.

OPPOSITE: The living room sits two steps lower than the rest of the first floor. The level change feels distinctly retro, creating a separation of spaces that is subtle and unobstructed.

We always knew the
dining table would
be round. Somehow
nostalgic, it brings us
back to family dinners,
board games, and
late-night laughs.

ABOVE: The kitchen window provides the very best winter light and a sweet view of the log cabin next door. The integrated bench seat with drawers is the best place for one of us to hang out while the other is cooking.

OPPOSITE: We wanted this kitchen to not only be beautiful, but functional too. The open shelving provides access to our most frequently used items, keeps the space feeling light, and contributes to that cabin feel.

OPPOSITE: This perspective is one of our favorites. We break up the oak with warm handmade brick tiles, and in the corner, a large pot is full of herbs for cooking.

ABOVE, LEFT: Oak on oak on oak. Here you can see the contrast between the white oak cabinetry and the red oak nickel-gap paneled walls.

ABOVE, RIGHT: At the time of writing this book, the kitchen was brand new. In the coming months, the brass will continue to patina, and the space will evolve to become uniquely ours.

Designing guest spaces can be tough
but rewarding. Anticipating the needs of
someone who may only stay the night,
we chose to prioritize comfort with king-
size beds and comfy linens.

The Maine loft, in many ways, is inspired
by a 1970s basement. This space is
somehow both bold and neutral at
the same time, and uniquely its own.
Undoubtedly, it is where we end each
day and catch up on our favorite show.

ABOVE: When we hung this collection of local maps, we thought to ourselves, "What if this whole wall was a map?!" The grid represents latitudinal and longitudinal lines, while a lighter (and difficult to capture in a photo) paint represents the topography of our area.

RIGHT: The view of the primary suite from the loft. This room, once much darker, is now bright with the addition of three skylights.

The goal in the primary suite was to create an
elevated retreat without losing the rustic charm of
a cabin in Maine.

We reconfigured the rough-sawn wood paneling so
that it wrapped and grounded the room. This allowed
us to go bold with the wallpaper, featuring mallards
like the ones you can find just outside.

STEPHEN KING
MR MERCEDES
LODGE

Views from bed—we don't close our curtains or blinds. Instead, we wake up each morning in a bright room, with views of the treetops.

We combined two smaller spaces to
create this primary bath. The theme was
light and bright, focusing on the view
outside and creating a contrast with the
saturated primary bedroom.

The natural surroundings of the Maine cabin are the primary feature. Our goal wasn't to design an experience, but rather to create moments for appreciating what already exists.

BRECK CABIN

In the summer of 2023, we spent six weeks in Breckenridge, Colorado, competing on HGTV's *Battle on the Mountain*. We had a $100,000 budget to create the winning renovation design for this chalet-style cabin. The home's character had always been there, hidden beneath years of neglect. Our goal was to balance rustic mountain charm with modern living in the heart of ski country.

Over a short period, we renovated the kitchen, living room, dining room, mudroom, three bedrooms, two bathrooms, and exterior—an enormous undertaking. Our greatest achievement was creating a home we were truly proud of, refusing to cut corners or make decisions we couldn't stand behind, and designing spaces we could genuinely see ourselves living in.

Royal

We worked quickly to add as much character as possible to the design. From the beginning, we developed a whole-home mood board and guidelines to ensure consistency throughout. This mudroom was created by reconfiguring the back of the home, using only salvaged lumber to form a functional, bright space—perfect for dropping ski gear after a day on the mountain.

In each space, we worked to create a moment. Here, Stephen's photograph of a nearby mountain—printed on vinyl with aluminum backing—adds a detail that anchors the bed in the room. Bespoke details make any space feel more special; they take effort and thoughtful intention that can't be bought.

With any destination home, it's important that families have space. We used the double-height areas to add room for sleeping or storage. This beautiful ladder was handmade by our carpenter, with art beside it purchased from a local artisan.

To add adventure, this mixed-use room features a queen bed, a working desk made of local live-edge wood, and a rock wall leading to the loft above. We were told the rock wall might be too scary for some kids, but the kids we know would be just fine.

Resources

Boston

PARLOR

Walls, Ceiling, Trim, and Bookcase:
Colonial Verdigris CW-530
Fabric: Ralph Lauren Gauciel Green FRL5204
Art: Pat Cantin
Bookcase Art: Artie B. Vanderpool

DINING ROOM

Paneling and Trim: Pure White SW 7005
Wallpaper: Cole & Son Florencecourt
Charcoal Wallpaper
Furnishings: Room & Board

KITCHEN

Walls: Alabaster SW 7008
Cabinets and Trim: Barbara (custom formula)
Cabinetry: Conestonga
Appliances: Fisher & Paykel
Stone: Vermont Imperial Danby Marble
Lighting and Hardware: Rejuvenation

LIVING ROOM

Walls and Trim: Narragansett Green HC-157
Ceiling: Pearly Star DE6268

ENTRY

Walls and Ceiling: Alabaster SW 7008
Floors: Quartersawn Oak with Minwax 50% Read Oak
and 50% Dark Walnut
Décor: Nancy Russell

PRIMARY BEDROOM

Walls: Elizabeth I by Portola Paints, Roman Clay
Trim: Paperclip C2-928
Bedroom Wallpaper: Grasscloth Sisal by Magnolia Home
Closet Wallpaper: Homestead by Magnolia Home

PRIMARY BATH

Walls: Elizabeth I by Portola Paints, Roman Clay
Trim: Paperclip C2-928
Tile: Firenze Carrara Honed Marble
Vanity: Room & Board
Hardware: Brizo

EXTERIOR

Shingle: Kendall Charcoal HC-116
Trim: Acadia White OC-38
Fence: Black Forest Green HC-187
Furnishings: Rejuvenation

COWBOY ROOM

Walls Upper and Trim: Horizon OC-53
Walls Lower: Metropolitan AF-690
Closet Doors: Urbane Bronze SW 7048

OFFICE & SNUG

Walls: Alabaster SW 7008
Millwork: Kuiken Brothers
Skylights: VELUX
Furnishings: AllModern

PRINCESS ROOM

Walls: Great White No.2006
Trim: Whisper White HDC-MD-08

Maine

PRIMARY BEDROOM

Ceiling and Skylights: Elemental AF-400

Wallpaper: Mulberry Grand Flying Ducks

Skylights: VELUX

PRIMARY BATHROOM

Walls and Ceiling: Lime White CW-95

Paneling and Trim: Tavern Gray CW-40

LIVING ROOM

Walls and Ceiling: Capital White CW-10

Baseboards: Dixon Brown CW-160

Furnishings: AllModern

PLAID ROOM

Trim: Narragansett Green HC-157

Ceiling: Capital White CW-10

Wallpaper: Check 11,5 by Coordonne

Millwork: V Joint Tongue & Groove Paneling
by Kuiken Brothers

Furnishings: AllModern

LOFT

Walls: Capital White CW-10

Furnishings: AllModern

KITCHEN

Walls: Red Oak Nickle Gap

Ceiling: Capital White CW-10

Cabinetry: White Oak by Block Brothers

Appliances: Fisher & Paykel

Stone: Black Pearl Granite Leathered

Lighting and Hardware: Rejuvenation

PANEL ROOM

Walls: Pine Tongue & Groove

Cciling: Capitol White CW-10

Breck

EXTERIOR

Dark Trim Color: Greenblack SW 6994

Light Trim Color: Shade-Grown SW 6188

LIVING ROOM

Rafters and Trim: Greenblack SW 6994

Fireplace: Elizabeth I by Portola Paints, Roman Clay

Floors (throughout): Camarilla Oak by Hallmark Floors

KITCHEN

Rafters and Trim: Greenblack SW 6994

Backsplash: Remedy in Herbal by Daltile

Counter: Black Pearl Granite Leathered

GUEST ROOM

Walls: Evergreen Fog SW 9130

BONUS ROOM

Rockwall: Labradorite SW 7619

Acknowledgments

To all of those who have followed along and contributed to our renovation journey—we thank you. Your encouragement, thoughtfulness, laughter, and love have transformed our lives in countless ways. This book is a love letter to you, and to all that we have created together.

To our parents, siblings, and grandparents: everything we have done, or could ever imagine achieving, is thanks to your unwavering support. Thank you for instilling in us the confidence to follow our dreams and the importance of dedication and hard work.

To our friends: thank you for your infectious enthusiasm whenever we tackle something new. Your kind words and love allow us to see through the weeds and appreciate the beauty in what we have created.

To the trades, makers, and real estate professionals who have supported us: thank you for helping us make our vision a reality.

To our book team, we extend our sincere gratitude. To our editor, Alexander Rigby, for believing that we had something meaningful to contribute and for providing us with this incredible opportunity. Your expert guidance transformed our little idea into a beautiful story of our journey and work. To Joanna Price, whose incredible design work is present throughout these pages. To Coy Sellers, for the amazing lifestyle photography that has contributed so much to our story. And finally, our assistant, Sinéad Slabine, deserves special recognition for reading thousands of drafts and being a constant source of light throughout this process.

Thank you all so, so much.

To my husband Stephen, thank you for waking me up each morning with a cup of coffee. Your contribution to my life over the past eighteen years is more than I could have hoped for over eighteen lifetimes. Creating with you is the best thing I've ever done—your incredible talent and dedication to capturing these creations is undoubtedly the reason we are here today.

—David

To David: While we have created many things together, the process of writing this book together has punctuated all the facets I adore about you. Putting our story to paper has been a gift of perspective. I appreciate you comprehensively. I'm so proud of the two boys who fell in love and decided to build this life together.

—Stephen

Index

About the Authors

David and Stephen St. Russell are a husband-and-husband design and DIY team with a passion for a good project. Together, they've renovated multiple homes—including their 1893 Boston Victorian and 1975 Maine cabin—documenting the process and building an incredible community along the way.

In 2024, they took the top prize on HGTV's *Battle on the Mountain* with their beautiful mountain home design. They have also been featured on Magnolia Network's *Diary of an Old Home*, and in 2022 won the Boston Preservation Achievement Award for their Victorian restoration.

David graduated from Springfield College where he studied medicine. Stephen graduated from Massachusetts College of Art and Design where he studied architecture. They have been together since 2008 and can be found online as the Renovation Husbands.